THE AUTHOR OF
HITLER AND NAZISM

Dr. Louis L. Snyder, Professor of History at City College of New York, is eminently suited to write the story of Adolf Hitler and his Nazis. As a German-American Exchange Fellow in 1928 at the University of Frankfort am Main, and as an Alexander von Humbolt-Stiftung Foundation Fellow in 1929–1930, he witnessed the Nazi mass meetings and S.A. demonstrations. As a result of his experiences as a student in Germany and of his discussions with fellow students, Dr. Snyder, in 1932, published his book **Hitlerism, The Iron Fist in Germany.** A full year before Hitler came to power, this book accurately predicted Hitler's rise, his alliance with Mussolini, the war with France, and the persecution of the Jews.

Dr. Snyder is the author of many books on modern European history, including **German Nationalism: The Tragedy of a People, Basic History of Modern Germany, The First Book of World War II, The War: A Concise History, 1939–1945,** and **The Military History of the Lusitania.**

HITLER AND NAZISM
by Louis L. Snyder

BANTAM BOOKS
TORONTO · NEW YORK · LONDON

This low-priced Bantam Book
has been completely reset in a type face
designed for easy reading, and was printed
from new plates. It contains the complete
text of the original hard-cover edition.
NOT ONE WORD HAS BEEN OMITTED.

HITLER AND NAZISM
A Bantam Book / published by arrangement with
Franklin Watts, Inc.

PRINTING HISTORY

Watts edition published March 1961
Seven printings through August 1966
Bantam edition / January 1967

2nd printing ... January 1967	4th printing ...... May 1968
3rd printing ...... May 1967	5th printing .... August 1971
6th printing .... June 1976	

7th printing

ISBN 0-553-08047-4

Published simultaneously in the United States and Canada

Bantam Books are published by Bantam Books, Inc. Its trade-
mark, consisting of the words "Bantam Books" and the por-
trayal of a bantam, is registered in the United States Patent
Office and in other countries. Marca Registrada. Bantam
Books, Inc., 666 Fifth Avenue, New York, New York 10019.

PRINTED IN THE UNITED STATES OF AMERICA

This book is for
Harvey Sacarob
and
Mal and Douglas Snyder

"This wicked man . . . this monstrous product
of former wrongs and shame . . ."
— WINSTON CHURCHILL

Contents

CHAPTER ONE 卐 卐 卐 卐 卐 卐 卐 卐 卐 卐 卐 卐 卐 卐 卐

The Birth of a Tyrant

ON April 20, 1889, in the small village of Braunau on the River Inn between Austria and Germany, a child was born to a strutting Austrian customs official of fifty-two and a peasant girl still in her twenties. The little boy was christened Adolf—an ordinary enough name for a most extraordinary baby. For this child, the third of his father's third unhappy marriage, would one day push himself to supreme power over the German people. Grown into a flabby, wild-eyed little man with an unruly forelock and a Charlie Chaplin mustache, he would bestride a continent, soak it in blood, and reduce it to misery and despair. It would take a great military offensive to strike him down. In the end, he would crawl into his Berlin bunker and shoot himself in the mouth.

The story of Adolf Hitler is not a pretty tale. There was almost nothing kind, romantic, or gentle about the life of this self-styled hero who said that he was the greatest German of all time. It is the story of an evil man. It is the story of a man who released on the world such plagues and misery as it had never known.

The future dictator of Germany was born of coarse peasant stock. Both sides of his family came from a country district called the *Waldviertel,* or Woodlands, of Lower Austria. In this back-country section of hills and woods there lived a hard-working community of small peasants. Most of them were poor. They raised potatoes, cut wood, burned charcoal, and tried to make a living on the barren land.

The people of the *Waldviertel* were as harsh as the land they inhabited. They were unfriendly, humorless, and sullen, quite unlike their merry neighbors nearby on the slopes of the Danube. They laughed little and worried much. They were suspicious of the city folk from Vienna, fifty miles away, and stayed close together. Many of them intermarried.

Hitler's grandfather, Johann Georg Hiedler, was a wandering peasant, moving from one village to another, working as a miller, grinding the grain brought to him by other peasants. One day he met a peasant girl named Maria Anna Schicklgruber. In 1837 Maria Anna gave birth to a son, Alois. Five years later, Johann and Maria Anna were married.

Until he was forty years old, Alois, Adolf Hitler's father, was known by his mother's name of Schicklgruber. He was reared in the house of his uncle, Johann Nepomuk Hiedler. In 1876 Johann Nepomuk gave his nephew a legitimate name. He had the parish priest cross out the word "illegitimate" on the church register and add a statement signed by witnesses that his brother, Johann Georg Hiedler, was the father of the child Alois.

Thus it was that twelve years before Adolf was born, his father began to call himself Hitler. What a stroke of fortune for the future dictator! Imagine mobs of obedient Germans shouting *"Heil* Schicklgruber!"

Boy Against Father

ADOLF HITLER'S mother, Klara Pölzl, was quiet, honest, hard-working, and respectable. Photographs show her with a solemn, pale face, and large, staring eyes. She kept the house shining clean and tried in every way to please her husband.

Adolf was her favorite child. He himself later said that he was "mother's darling." He probably loved her as much as he was capable of loving anyone, but he used her to get his own way. He had no trouble forcing his will on her because she, in turn, loved him, even if, as she said, he was "moon-struck." She always told him how different he was from other children. Despite her love, she made him into a resentful and unhappy child. In a way, she was making him, and through him the world, pay for her own unhappiness with her husband.

Adolf's father was a hard, difficult man. A tyrant at heart, he no doubt set the pattern for Adolf's own brutal view of life. Alois liked to strut around in his border policeman's uniform with its shiny gold buttons and gold-rimmed velvet cap. The pistol at his belt gave him a sense of power. When he was fifty-six, he retired on a pension.

Fifty-six is a young age at which to stop work. Alois Hitler did not seem to know what to do with himself. He raised bees, bought and sold farms, and did whatever he could to pass the time. But he spent most of his time at the village inn, drinking and brooding and boasting. His comrades there did not like him very much.

3

Alois Hitler was just a miserable, lonely man. He had had three unhappy marriages. He believed he could drown his memories in alcohol, but it never seemed to work. People laughed at him behind his back. Many a time the young Hitler had to help carry his tipsy father home.

This sour, obstinate, hot-tempered man was master inside his home. What he said was law. No child could ever speak back to him. All the children, but especially Adolf, felt their father's cane, switch, dog-whip, and belt.

Between father and son there was a continuous battle. One reason for it may have been the great difference in their ages. When Adolf was 6, his father was 58. When Adolf was 12, his father was 64. At the thought of facing the anger of what must have seemed to him a very old man, the lad was often afraid to step inside his house. Alois snarled at him, humiliated him, and corrected him over and over again. Sometimes the boy reacted violently. There were two fierce, unbending wills in conflict.

Most of all, father and son clashed on Adolf's future. Alois wanted the boy to be a civil servant. After all, if that job was good enough for him it was good enough for his son. But Adolf would not hear of it. One day he told his father that he wanted to become an artist.

"No! No! No!" said his father. "*Never*, as long as I live!"

Soon after, Adolf discovered a weapon he could use against his father. He had been beaten by the old man many times. He would pay him back by failing in school. He would be lazy, sick, a failure. It would serve his father right to have a son who had to repeat a year in school.

This tension between father and son was a serious thing. No doubt Adolf Hitler's later passionate hatreds came in part from his deep hostility to his father. Also, his father's harsh treatment gave Adolf the idea that right is always on the side of the stronger.

Millions of innocent people would suffer and die because of the unhappiness of this strong-willed boy.

Education of a Dictator

JUST before he was six years old, Adolf entered the public school in the village of Fischlham. Two years later he was sent to the monastery school at Lambach. Frau Hitler, a highly religious woman, wanted her boy to become a monk. But Adolf had other ideas. One day he was surprised in the act of smoking a cigarette in the monastery gardens. The outraged monks expelled him. That was the end of Adolf's religious life.

Soon after that, Adolf's father moved the family to Leonding, a small suburb of Linz. During his first five years in the town, Adolf did well in school. Most of his marks were "excellent." And in some ways he enjoyed himself. He was a mischievous boy, with a fondness for practical jokes. He and his gleeful fellow pupils overturned washing troughs and sent them sailing down the stream.

Adolf joined the boys' gangs. He led the "Indians" of his town against the "Trappers" of the next Austrian village. He brought knives and axes to school to trade with his comrades. He was full of plans for running away from home and taking a trip around the world.

Above all, Adolf liked to play "Follow the Leader." And he was always the leader.

After grammar school came high school. There were two kinds of high school in Austria—the *Gymnasium*, which stressed mainly the arts, and the *Realschule*, devoted mostly to the sciences. Adolf wanted to go to the

Gymnasium, but this was the school of the upper classes. His father wanted him to go to the *Realschule* because he felt it to be more suitable and practical and not too "intellectual." The *Gymnasium,* he said, was for doctors, lawyers, and professors.

Adolf went to the *Realschule* because his father wanted it. But he failed his first year and had to repeat it. About this time young Adolf changed from a smart, wide-awake boy into a serious, silent, gloomy young man.

Adolf was 13 when the struggle with his father came to an end. Alois Hitler was in an inn talking to a friend when suddenly he fell to the floor. Blood filled his mouth. A doctor was called, but it was too late. Alois Hitler had died of a lung ailment. They buried him in his gold-braided uniform.

After the death of his father, Adolf was transferred from Linz to the state high school at Steyr. This was a modern city where bicycles, automobiles, and armaments were made. The artistic Adolf felt better here. He liked the buildings, and felt free to sketch them as much as he wanted. He no longer had to worry about being beaten by his father.

But Adolf was still lazy in his schoolwork. In the school record there were such entries as: "Hilter was late," "Hitler disturbed the lecture," or "Hitler forgot his notebook again."

The boy studied only when he felt like it. "The things which pleased me, I learned," he wrote later. "Above all, everything that I thought would be of use to me later as a painter. The things that seemed to me meaningless in this respect or which did not appeal to me, I sabotaged completely. My report at this time presented extremes."

The studies that "pleased" him were drawing, gymnastics, and history. The things he did not like made a longer list: mathematics, German, chemistry, religion, physics, and stenography.

Adolf Hitler's last school report for the fourth class was issued on September 16, 1905:

ADOLF HITLER

STUDENT IN THE FOURTH CLASS

	First Semester	Second Semester
DEPORTMENT	Satisfactory	Satisfactory
INDUSTRY	Uneven	Satisfactory
RELIGION	Fair	Satisfactory
GERMAN LANGUAGE	Unsatisfactory	Fair
GEOGRAPHY, HISTORY	Fair	Satisfactory
MATHEMATICS	Unsatisfactory	Satisfactory
CHEMISTRY	Fair	Fair
PHYSICS	Satisfactory	Fair
GEOMETRY	Fair	Unsatisfactory
FREEHAND DRAWING	Praiseworthy	Excellent
CALISTHENICS	Excellent	Excellent
STENOGRAPHY	Unsatisfactory	(Dropped)
SINGING	(Not attended)	Satisfactory
PENMANSHIP	Disagreeable	Disagreeable

Adolf quit school without being graduated. He was almost 16 years old. He was so happy that he would never again have to go to school that, for the first time in his life, he drank himself into a stupor. After that he never touched alcohol.

For three years Adolf did nothing. He stayed at home most of the time. Sometimes he roamed the streets. He would sit for hours in the public library reading German history or mythology. Somehow, it was always Germany, not his own country, Austria, that attracted him most.

Little by little he lost contact with other boys of his age. He kept out of the way of anyone who had an education. Educated people reminded him too much of his hated school life.

In later years Hitler blamed his lack of learning not on himself but on his teachers. "Most of my teachers," he said, "had something wrong with them mentally, and quite a few of them ended their days as honest-to-God lunatics."

But there was one teacher who was different. His name was Dr. Leopold Poetsch. "It was perhaps decisive for my whole later life," Hitler once said, "that good fortune gave me this teacher, who made history my favorite subject."

Dr. Poetsch was a Pan-Germanist; that is to say, he believed all Germans, no matter where they lived, should be united into one nation. From him the youthful Hitler began to learn the meaning of German patriotism. He also learned to despise the rulers of his own country, the Hapsburgs, because they lacked a sense of *German* nationalism.

Love for Germany and all things German became a driving force in Adolf Hitler's life. It offers a key to some of his actions as dictator.

CHAPTER FOUR 卐卐卐卐卐卐卐卐卐卐卐卐卐卐卐卐卐

Flophouse Artist in Vienna

In October 1907, when he was just 18 years old, Adolf Hitler came to Vienna. Supported by money sent by his mother, he had hopes of becoming a great artist.

Then there came a terrible blow. To become a student in the Vienna Academy of Fine Arts, Hitler had to submit several drawings. If his drawings were accepted, he could take the regular tests. But twice his drawings were rejected. Crude, weak, without life, they were just not good enough.

Hitler never recovered from this blow to his pride. He blamed not himself but "the stupid professors" for not seeing that he was a fine artist.

Late in December, 1908, Hitler's mother died. Though she had been sick for a long time, the young man hurried home only for the funeral. He was crushed. The death of his mother meant that he had to find some way of earning his own living. He did not want to be a laborer, nor did he want to be an office worker. He just wanted to be an artist—and there was little chance for that now.

The next five years, according to Hitler, were the most miserable of his life. "I lived five years of misery and woe in Vienna," he wrote. "Five years, in which I earned my living first as apprentice and then as unknown painter. My truly sparing bread was never enough to appease even an ordinary hunger. This hunger was my faithful companion. It never left me for a moment. Every book I got; every visit to the opera; everything was done at the expense of this hunger. My life was a continual struggle with this pitiless friend."

At this time Hitler made little drawings or water colors on post cards. He drew poster advertisements and cards to be framed. Most of them were stiff views of Viennese buildings. He found it difficult to draw human figures or even heads.

Hitler daily made the rounds of the cafés and picture framers, trying to sell his drawings so that he could eat. Those who knew him in Vienna at that time say that he looked like an untidy vagabond. He was never properly shaved. He wore a filthy black derby and a long overcoat that reached to his ankles. He had picked the overcoat up from an old clothes dealer, a Hungarian Jew.

In November, 1909, Hitler had to leave his rooming house because he had no more money. For a time he slept in cafés or on park benches. Then he went to a "flophouse," where vagabonds could sleep for a few pennies. Each day he joined the lines of needy people waiting for free soup. He did all sorts of odd jobs. Sometimes he shoveled snow on the bridges, carried bags outside railway stations, or beat carpets.

On the whole, however, Adolf avoided heavy physical work. He told himself that he was sickly and fragile and should not strain himself. More, he felt that if he got into the habit of doing manual labor, he would never do anything else.

Unlike his fellow vagabonds, Hitler never smoked because of his bad lungs. He never drank alcohol, probably as a protest against his father, who drank too much. Nor would he have anything to do with women. Poor and unwashed, he was, indeed, an unattractive figure.

Hitler hated Vienna. But he came there half a boy, and left it a man.

"In this period, there took shape within me a world picture and a philosophy which became the granite foundation of all my acts."

It was in Vienna that Hilter learned to hate.

First, he learned to hate the Socialists, those who wanted a society ruled by the working class. He studied Karl Marx, father of socialism, but violently rejected his teachings. The way to treat Socialists, he decided, was to strike back at them with equal or greater power. If the workers used terror in the workshops, factories, at meetings, and on the streets, he felt that they should be hit with an equally violent terror.

Second, Hitler learned to hate the Jews. As a youth he had never even heard the word "Jew." There had been only a few Jews in Linz. But in Vienna he began to read anti-Jewish magazines and hate-literature.

One day on a street in Vienna he saw a Jew in a caftan, a long-sleeved gown fastened by a girdle.

"I asked myself, could this be a German?"

Then followed what Hitler called a soul-tearing battle between "feeling and reason." At last he decided that the Jew was not a German, but of another "race' altogether.

In Austria, Jews held high positions in business, medicine, law, and journalism. Hitler believed this would ruin Austria. He decided that Marxists and Jews were in "a holy union" to destroy the world.

"If the Jew wins over the world with the help of Marxist doctrines," he said, "then this crown will be the wreath of death for mankind. So I believe in the spirit of the Almighty Creator. I shall defend myself against the Jew. I shall fight for the work of the Lord!"

From that time on Hitler attacked the Jews as "dirty rats," "parasites," "bloodsuckers," "tyrants." He turned the full force of his hatred on the Jews. It was easy to blame the other fellow for his own misery.

It was while he was in Vienna that Hitler began to despise democracy. He scorned the Hapsburg family who ruled the Austrians, and he mocked the parliament that was supposed to represent the people. His queer, tortured mind found relief in dreams of a great and glorious Germany. The day would come, he told himself, when the Germans would take over this weak Austrian state.

Slowly, Hitler began to believe that he was the child of fate. Germany needed a guiding hand. Perhaps he was destined to be that strong hand!

Hitler visited the cheap cafés and started political arguments. As soon as anyone mentioned politics he was off on a long speech. If anyone spoke against him, he would react violently by screaming at the top of his voice.

And a strange thing happened. People began to listen to this sickly, harried young man with the hypnotic eyes.

Hitler left Vienna in May, 1913. He had failed in the big city. He had no money, no family, no friends. He was unwanted and unloved. But he had made a discovery about himself: he could make people listen when he talked.

What should he do now? He would leave the land of his father and go to the land that he loved—Germany. He went from Vienna to Munich—from Austria, where he had failed, to Germany, where he might possibly find a happy future.

After all, Munich was a *German* city! That would make a difference. In Munich, Hitler's ideas became fixed. He began to feel that the German government was entirely wrong in its foreign policy. The Triple Alliance— Germany, Austria-Hungary, and Italy—would never stick together, he said, and he was right. The Slavs in Austria-Hungary and the Italians would both defect in case of war, he warned. Germany should break up the alliance, make friends with England, and turn on Russia.

In Munich, too, Hitler was depressed, embittered. Here, again, he was the lonely stranger in a gay, throbbing city.

The Good Soldier Adolf

THE START of World War I changed Hitler's life. Later he said, "The war came as a deliverance from the distress that had weighed upon me during the days of my youth. Overpowered by stormy enthusiasm, I fell upon my knees and thanked Heaven from an overflowing heart."

Six months earlier Hitler had gone to an Austrian border city to take a physical examination for the army service that was demanded of all able-bodied young men. The examination was three years overdue, and he had been marked on the rolls as a deserter. But now the doctor said, "Too weak; unfit to bear arms."

Hitler was delighted. He did not want to serve Austria. He wanted to be a German! He wrote to the King of Bavaria, one of the large South German states, and asked to serve in the Bavarian army. He was assigned to the 16th Bavarian Infantry Regiment, also called the List Regiment. It was composed of student volunteers.

After only a few weeks' training, Hitler was sent to the front. He proved himself a brave and able soldier. Until 1916 he served as an orderly for Lieutenant-Colonel Tubeuf of the List Regiment, and later as a dispatch bearer. During his four years on the Western Front he took part in forty-eight battles. Often he was in the thick of the fighting. Again and again he had the good luck to be spared by the bursting shells as he ran through the scarred land carrying his messages.

Hitler was wounded twice and decorated several times. On October 7, 1916, he was brought to the hospital at Hermis with a wounded leg. In March of the next year he was again in the combat zones. He took part in the first two great German offensives.

On October 14, 1918, just three weeks before the end of the war, Hitler was badly gassed. He was sent to the rear and at last reached a military hospital at Pasewalk, a small town near Berlin. There he spent months in agony, his eyes burning like live coals. At first the doctors had no hope of saving his sight, but slowly he improved.

Hitler received his first decoration, the Iron Cross, second class, in 1914. On August 4, 1918, he was awarded the Iron Cross, first class. It was a rare award for a common soldier in the old German Imperial Army. Hitler was given this medal because it was said that he had captured an enemy officer and about fifteen men, and led them to his regimental staff.

If Hitler was a brave and able soldier, why was he not promoted beyond lance corporal? One of his superior officers later said that he was so good a dispatch bearer that no officer wanted to lose him by promoting him. Another officer did not agree. He said Hitler was too mentally unstable to be promoted.

During his war days, Hitler made few friends among his fellow soldiers. Most of them resented his long political harangues. "We all cursed him, and couldn't stand him," said one of them later. Another said, "We lived on our bellies, he on his nerves."

Unlike most of his comrades, Hitler *enjoyed* the cruel business of war. He never grumbled or griped or spoke about going home. He hated the enemy and longed to defeat him. The killing that went on around him did not sicken him at all. In all probability his hatreds were stimulated during the war years.

On Sunday morning, November 10, 1918, a pastor came through the hospital ward bearing important news. The Kaiser had abdicated! The German Republic had been proclaimed! The war was over!

Many of the wounded men breathed a sigh of relief, but not the half-blinded Hitler. He was crushed. As he later said, "Since the day when I stood beside the grave of my mother, I had not cried. It appeared to me almost a sin to grieve when so many dear comrades and friends were called out of the ranks by death. They died for Germany.

"And as the creeping gas began to eat into my eyes during the last days of the war, and as I began to weaken under the terror of blindness—but for a moment—then a voice thundered, 'Miserable fool, you want to weep while thousands are worse off than you.'

"The more I tried to understand the great events of this hour, the more my brow burned with shame.

"What followed were terrible days and even worse nights. I knew that everything was lost. Only fools—or liars or criminals—could hope for mercy from the enemy. In these nights my hate grew against the men who had brought about this crime.

"I, however, decided to go into politics."

Hitler Creates the Nazi Party

In the summer of 1919, Hitler became member number 7 of a small group of restless men called the German Workers' Party. The party had no program, no plan of action. It was just "against" the government. It had only seven and a half marks (less than $2.00) in its treasury.

It was not long before Hitler was the leader of this party. It was like Linz all over again—he, Adolf, was the natural leader of the boys. The group held its meetings in the back room of a Munich café. Here Hitler discovered once more his talent as an orator.

"I could speak!" he later wrote. "After thirty minutes the people in the tiny room were electrified."

From that time on Hitler lost no chance to talk before a crowd wherever he could find one. He seemed intoxicated by his own voice. He liked to denounce the Treaty of Versailles—the peace treaty after World War I, which, he said, caused all Germany's troubles. He played on the emotions of his listeners until, in his own words, "I had before me a surging mass full of sacred, boundless wrath."

Within two years Hitler had blown up the little party into a big one. He changed its name. It was now called the National Socialist German Workers' Party, or the N.S.D.A.P., after its German initials. The word Nazi came from the first two words of the German name— *NAtional SoZIalist.*

All kinds of discontented people flocked to the new party. There were war veterans, poor students, monarchists, who wanted the Hohenzollern emperors back again, struggling shopkeepers, unhappy workers, frightened businessmen, anti-Semites, anti-Catholics, anti-liberals, anti-Socialists, and anti-Communists. All joined Hitler because he gave them hope by promising them a better life.

On February 25, 1920, Hitler announced his program of twenty-five points. It was cleverly designed to appeal to almost everybody.

1. We demand the union of all Germans in a Great Germany.

2. We demand the end of the Treaty of Versailles.

3. We demand colonies for settling our surplus population.

4. Only those of German blood can be citizens. No Jew, therefore, can be a member of the nation.

5. Any non-citizen may live in Germany only as a guest.

6. Only citizens can vote.

7. The first duty of the State is to promote the well-being of its citizens. If it is not possible to nourish all the people, then non-citizens are to be excluded.

8. All non-Germans who came into Germany after August 2, 1914, shall be deported at once.

9. All citizens of the State shall enjoy equal rights and duties.

10. The first duty of a citizen is to work for the common good.

11. We demand the end of all income unearned by work or effort. (This meant, for example, any interest on bank accounts.)

12. We demand that all war profits be taken over by the State.

13. We demand that the State take over all large businesses, such as trusts.

14. We demand profit sharing in large concerns.

15. We demand old age pensions.

16. We demand a healthy middle class.

17. We demand land reform.

18. We demand a ruthless struggle against profiteers, who must be punished with death.

19. We demand that the Roman law be replaced by German law.

20. We demand that our whole system of education be revised.

21. The State must provide for improvement of public health by protecting mothers and children, ending child labor, and supporting health education for the young.

22. We demand the formation of a national army.

23. We demand an end to the lying press.

24. We demand religious freedom, in so far as any religion does not work against the State.

25. To carry out these demands we call for the creation of a strong central authority in the Reich. The leaders of the Party promise that they will fight to the death for this program.

A few months later the leaders of the Nazi Party declared that, "This program is never to be changed."

With his program set, Hitler now began to organize his followers. He gave the Party a flag of its own. With funds rolling in, he also bought a newspaper for the Party—the *Völkischer Beobachter* or *People's Observer*.

What Hitler needed most of all was a trained militia that would guard his meetings. He had to have shock troops to evict hecklers. He wanted good fighters for the street brawls with his enemies.

For this purpose Hitler organized the Brown Shirts, called the S.A., after *Sturmabteilung,* or storm detachment. He named Captain Ernst Röhm, one of his closest friends, to lead these street bullies.

The second group, called the S.S., from *Schutzstaffeln,* or defense corps, was a small, highly disciplined personal bodyguard for Hitler himself. These so-called "elite soldiers" wore black shirts, a death's head insignia, and carried daggers. They were pledged to fight to the death for Hitler.

Hitler gave his followers a good show. He chose red as the basic color for the party's flag, partly because he wanted to annoy the Socialists and Communists by using their favorite color. He placed a black swastika on a white circle and thereby restored the old colors of the Empire—black, white, and red. The red field meant anti-capitalism;

the white circle meant nationalism; and the black hooked-cross, the swastika, meant the superiority of the "Aryan race."

Hitler outfitted his Nazis in flashy uniforms. He gave them dozens of medals and pins and decorations. Knowing they loved parades, he kept them marching and drilling day and night. The official Nazi song was written by a young street fighter of low reputation named Horst Wessel who died a violent death and was made a national hero by Hitler. Here is part of the *Horst Wessel Song:*

Hold high the banner! Close the hard ranks serried!
S.A. marches on with sturdy stride.
Comrades by Red Front and Reaction killed, are buried,
But march with us in image at our side.

Gangway! Gangway now for the Brown Battalions!
For the Storm Trooper clear roads o'er the land!
The Swastika gives hope for our entranced millions,
The day for freedom and for bread's at hand.

Another favored song of the Nazis was *Deutschland Erwache:*

GERMANY, AWAKE!
Storm, storm, storm, storm!
From tower to tower peal bells of alarm.
Peal out! Sparks fly as hammers strike.
Come Judas forth to win the Reich.
Peal out! The bloody ropes hang red.
Around our martyred hero dead.
Peal out—that thundering earth may know
Salvation's rage for honor's sake.
To people dreaming still comes woe.
Germany awake! Awake!

And this song was sung against the Communists in the deadly battle of the streets:

The red brood, beat them to a pulp!

Storm troops are on the march—clear the way!

There were also songs about "Jewish blood spurting under the knife." The Nazis screamed their slogans through all Germany:

GERMANY, AWAKE!
THE JEWS ARE OUR MISFORTUNE!
DOWN WITH THE CATHOLICS!
LONG LIVE OUR GLORIOUS *FUEHRER!*
TODAY GERMANY, TOMORROW THE WORLD!

CHAPTER SEVEN

The Beer Hall Putsch, November 8, 1923

THE *Bürgerbräu Keller* was one of the largest beer halls in Munich. Here thousands of thirsty Germans gathered during the evenings to drink beer out of stone mugs and to sing rousing drinking songs. Great political rallies were also held in these halls.

On the evening of November 8, 1923, some three thousand people were gathered in the *Bürgerbräu Keller* to hear a speech by Gustav von Kahr, State Commissioner of Bavaria. The other two rulers were General Otto von Lossow, commander of the German armed forces in Bavaria, and Colonel Hans von Seisser, head of the Bavarian secret police. In the audience that night were the most important leaders of Bavarian society—the government, army, business—the entire state power of Bavaria.

The crowd did not know that this was to be a most dramatic evening. They did not know that Adolf Hitler, leader of the Nazis, was going to try and take over control of the Bavarian government at one stroke, in what the Germans call a *putsch,* a petty rebellion or popular uprising.

The Nazis planned their attack well. In the darkness the six hundred storm troopers surrounded the beer hall. A machine gun was set up with its mouth pointed at the door from outside the hall. Someone slammed the door shut from the inside.

Von Kahr had been droning away at his speech for a

good half hour, and many in the audience were nodding sleepily. It had been a dull evening.

Then suddenly the front door opened, and down the aisle came a wildly excited little man with an oddly assorted group of followers. It was Adolf Hitler, surrounded by his cronies, who included Hermann Goering, Alfred Rosenberg, Rudolf Hess, and Ulrich Graf, and a huge, broad-shouldered butcher and wrestler who followed Hitler around like a faithful dog.

Hitler, in wild agitation, jumped on a chair, fired a pistol at the ceiling, and then in the sudden silence strode to the platform. He pushed the amazed von Kahr aside. Then, with eyes flashing, he yelled at the top of his voice, "The national revolution has broken out! The hall is filled with six hundred armed men. Nobody is allowed to leave. The Bavarian government and the government at Berlin are deposed. A new government will be formed at once. The barracks of the *Reichswehr* (the national army) and those of the police are occupied. Both have rallied to the swastika!"

The last sentences were barefaced lies. Neither the army nor the police was on Hitler's side. It was a daring bluff, but it worked.

The Nazi Party had been founded only three years before. It had only three delegates in the *Reichstag,* the German Congress. But already the Nazis were being led into revolution by the fiery Hitler.

In a loud voice Hitler ordered von Kahr, von Lossow, and von Seisser to follow him to a small side room. Dazed, they obeyed. He then began to lecture them. He was forming a new government with the war hero General Erich Ludendorff, he said, blandly ignoring the fact that the general, at this point, did not know that his name was being used. Then Hitler added that the three in the room would go along with him, or he would shoot them.

The three men were nervous, but by this time they had begun to recover their courage. They were not afraid of this ridiculous upstart. They started to denounce him. What did he mean by this confounded nonsense?

Hitler flew into a rage.

Meanwhile, outside in the hall, Goering was telling the

people to be quiet and drink their beer. The matter would be settled soon, he said. At the doors and windows tough storm troopers stood guard with pistols, rifles, and daggers.

Hitler dashed back into the hall, and shouted to the crowd, "Tomorrow will find a national government in Germany, or it will find us dead."

He yelled that the three Bavarian leaders had agreed to go along with the revolution. Again he lied. The audience cheered.

At this critical moment General Ludendorff arrived. Hitler had been careful to send for him, for he guessed that the general would be on his side. In fact, the old war horse had only contempt for the Weimar Republic, set up in 1919. Ludendorff hated democracy.

But General Ludendorff was furious with Hitler for starting the revolution without letting him know. What a stupid thing to do—to start a *putsch* in a beer hall! It was too late, however, to turn back. Ludendorff agreed to meet the Bavarian leaders, now Hitler's prisoners, in the back room. He seemed to win them over quickly.

All returned to the platform. Von Kahr, von Lossow, and von Seisser spoke briefly, as did Ludendorff. They swore loyalty to the new regime.

Beaming with joy, Hitler told the crowd that at last he had fulfilled "the oath I swore five years ago as a blind cripple in the military hospital."

An eyewitness later said that Hitler showed "insane excitement."

The great crowd had come to hear a set of boring speeches. Now it was seeing history made before its eyes. At first the thousands present had been hostile to the excitable little man with the mustache. Now they jumped up and onto the beer tables in a frenzy of enthusiasm.

All through the night a bitter struggle for power went on. One by one von Kahr, von Lossow, and von Seisser managed to sneak away. When the news was flashed back to Berlin that a *putsch* was under way in Munich, General Hans von Seeckt, commander of the *Reichswehr*, sent word that he himself would smash the rebellion if Munich could not do it.

Early the next morning Hitler began to realize that,

despite everything, he had failed. His spirits were crushed; he wanted to call off the whole thing. He suggested to General Ludendorff that the 3,000 storm troopers then in Munich be sent to the countryside to avoid further trouble.

But the hard-bitten old general would not hear of it. What, retreat? No, *he* would not retreat! *He* would lead the storm troopers in a march and take over the city.

"They will fire on us," said Hitler.

"We will march!" was Ludendorff's reply.

There was nothing Hitler could say. After all, this was a German general speaking to a lowly lance corporal.

At 11 A.M. on that gray morning, November 9, Nazi storm troopers, bearing huge swastika flags and war banners, marched toward the Marienplatz in the center of Munich. They pushed aside the small police squads that tried to bar the way.

At the head of the marchers were Ludendorff, Hitler, Goering, and Julius Streicher, bullet-headed, anti-Semitic agitator. Hitler carried a pistol. The storm troopers sang Nazi songs at the top of their voices.

As the parade came to the Odeonplatz near the Feldherrnhalle, a hall that honored the military heroes of German history, the way was barred by a detachment of police holding carbines. For a moment the two groups stared at one another—one hundred police against three thousand Nazis.

Hitler cried: "Surrender! Surrender!"

The answer was a hail of lead.

Within the space of a minute, sixteen Nazis and three policemen lay dead or dying on the pavement. Scores of others were wounded. Goering fell, shot through the thigh. He was taken to a building where a Jewish banker gave him first aid.

Hitler, the dispatch bearer of World War I, instinctively hit the ground as soon as he heard the crack of the guns. The act was fast enough to save his life, but he did hurt his shoulder. He got up quickly, and was rushed to one of the cars at the end of the column.

And what about the scowling, old General Ludendorff when the rifles cracked? Like a fearless Siegfried, his eyes straight ahead, he marched right through the ranks of the police. Someone yelled: "Don't shoot, His Excellency Ludendorff is coming!"

The term "His Excellency" had a magic effect in Germany. The police respectfully turned their guns aside and allowed the wartime general to go through their ranks to the open square.

Not a single Nazi followed him. What might have happened if others, including Hitler, had stayed at Ludendorff's side?

Both the police and the marchers, shocked by the bloodshed, stopped shooting.

Thus the Hitler *putsch* ended in a fiasco. But the Nazi movement had gotten its baptism of blood on the streets of Munich. There was more to follow.

Hitler was driven to the country home of one of his followers. Here he hid out for several days, quickly forgetting his promise to kill himself if the *putsch* failed.

CHAPTER EIGHT

In Jail at Landsberg

THREE DAYS after the beer hall *putsch* in Munich misfired, Hitler was arrested, put into prison, and charged with treason. His Nazi Party headquarters were raided, its literature seized, and its treasury impounded. The *Völkischer Beobachter,* the Nazi newspaper, was banned. Leading Nazis who had not already fled were thrown into jail.

In prison, Hitler began a hunger strike. For twelve days he refused to eat anything. But his cronies worked on him, building up his ego, telling him what a great man he was, promising that the Party would be born again. His appetite came back.

The trial began on February 26, 1924 in the *Kriegschule,* an old, red brick building in an officer's training school in the suburbs of Munich. In the prisoner's dock were Ludendorff, Frick, Röhm, Hess, Hitler, and others.

Hitler, acting as his own lawyer, put on a dazzling display of oratory. He admitted that he was the only one who had planned the *putsch.* He confessed that he wanted to overthrow the republic. He said that he had done only what von Kahr, von Lossow, and von Seisser, the dictators of Bavaria, had wanted to do themselves.

In court were a hundred reporters representing all the continents. Hitler gathered more and more courage and self-confidence as his words flew around the world. Inside Germany the people began to regard him as a great national hero and a patriot who wanted only good for Germany.

"This is my attitude," Hitler told his judges. "I would rather be hanged in a Bolshevist Germany than perish under the rule of French swords."

He was then asked by the court: by what right did he, a man almost without education, want to govern Germany, while sweeping aside all generals, presidents, and excellencies? Hitler replied that when a man knows that he can do a thing, he has to do it. "A bird must sing because it is a bird. A man who is born to be a dictator has a right to step forward."

Fully conscious of his world-wide audience, Hitler shouted in the courtroom that the hour would come when the masses, who stood on the streets with their swastika banners, would unite with those who would fire on them. "The army we have formed is growing day by day. One day these wild companies will grow into battalions, the battalions into regiments, the regiments into divisions. The old colors will then be rescued from the filth."

Hitler ended his harangue as if he were talking to a mass meeting: "I know the verdict that you are going to give. But the eternal court of history will not ask us: have you committed treason or not? Even if you judge us guilty a thousand times, the goddess of the eternal court of history will laugh at the motion of the federal attorney and she will tear up the verdict of this court, for she pronounces us not guilty."

The verdict of the judges was a mild one. Despite the bloody results of his *putsch,* Hitler was sentenced to only five years in prison.

Ludendorff, the old and revered war general, was acquitted. Röhm and Frick, though found guilty, were released. Hitler, together with Rudolf Hess, was sent to the prison at Landsberg on the Lech. It was more of a sanitarium than a prison.

Here Hitler served only eight and a half months of his term. He settled down in a comfortable cell and began to ponder on his mistakes. What had gone wrong? Why did the *putsch* fail just when everything seemed to be going well?

He decided that he had made two blunders. First, he had moved too quickly, before he had enough money and power behind him. Second, he had placed his hopes for success on conspiracy and other means outside the law. He saw now that a *putsch* was not the right way because it could not arouse the support of the more respectable and important circles of the German people. In order to win Germany he must use strictly "legal" means. That was it! *Strictly legal.* He must not use violence to get power. He must win the votes of the people. He must get them to *choose* him as dictator. He must get the German people to impose a tyranny upon themselves.

This was the lesson Hitler learned from his ill-fated Munich beer hall *putsch.* And, in fact, when he did come to power, he did so in strictly legal fashion. It was in accord with the Weimar Constitution, without violence or rebellion. By this time the German people were calling him *"Adolf Legalité,"* or "Adolf the Legal One."

To while away the hours in Landsberg prison, Hitler decided that he would write a book that could be used as a kind of guide by his followers. He began to dictate, first to several other prisoners, and lastly to Rudolf Hess, a book about his life and struggles. Because he liked to talk and could talk by the hour, the book soon grew to a size of almost eight hundred pages.

At first Hitler wanted to call his book: *Four and a Half Years of Struggle Against Lies, Stupidity, and Cowardice.* That gives a small idea of what Hitler thought of his many enemies. This was an imposing and impossible title, and a clever publisher decided to call it *Mein Kampf,* My Battle.

It is hard to imagine a worse book—from any point of view. In the first edition the writing was that of the jargon of Viennese tramps. Thousands of words were misspelled. In later editions the spelling was cleaned up, but the style remained grotesque, full of babblings, historical errors, plain lies. Whatever sense came out of the book was put into it by Rudolf Hess, who had more education than his Austrian comrade.

The theme of *Mein Kampf* was this: "Everybody keep silent. I alone am right. Listen to me."

It was truly a dull and boring book, and it was difficult to read. Here is a typical sentence:

At all times the driving changes in this world have been found less in a scientific knowledge animating the masses, but rather in a fanaticism dominating them and in a hysteria which drives them forward.

What Hitler was trying to say was this: "The masses of people do not reason. Like animals they are driven forward by fanaticism and hysteria." He was trying to show why it was necessary for a dictator to drive the masses with a whip. Thus, before he even came to power, Hitler revealed to the German people his contempt for democracy.

One critic called *Mein Kampf*—the Bible of the Nazi faith—"a queer mélange of half-truths and nonsense, combined with an almost uncanny insight into the mind of the mob." And again: "It is wordy, turgid, repetitious, ill-written; but it does throw light on Hitler, his aims, methods, character."

This was, however, a most important book in world history. Here was Hitler's criticism of Germany's policy, a manual of faith, a political testament. He never changed it. This was his blueprint for the kind of Germany, the kind of Europe, and the kind of world he intended to create. Few believed him at that time.

At first *Mein Kampf* sold very few copies. The intelligent German reading public looked upon it as the work of a crackpot. But slowly, as the Nazi movement gathered strength, the sales of the giant book began to get larger and larger.

Eventually *Mein Kampf* became a best seller. It went through many scores of German editions. By 1939 it had been translated into eleven languages, and more than 5,200,000 copies had been sold. As chancellor, Hitler decreed that every couple must buy a copy when they married. Boys and girls on their birthdays and old people on their anniversaries received copies as gifts.

Few people read *Mein Kampf*, but millions bought it. In the vast prison house that was Nazi Germany it was wise for every person to have a copy and to display it in the parlor.

From the sales of this book, Hitler became a rich man. The book netted him about $3,000,000. In 1939 his royalties from foreign sales alone amounted to $150,-000. Never in the history of literature has so bad a book been bought by so many and read by so few.

CHAPTER NINE 𝍢𝍢𝍢𝍢𝍢𝍢𝍢𝍢𝍢𝍢𝍢𝍢𝍢𝍢𝍢

The Strange Death of Geli Raubal

IN 1925, when his Nazi Party was striving for power, Hitler lived in a little house on the Obersalzberg above the village of Berchtesgaden near the Austrian border. At this time he arranged for his widowed half sister, Angela Raubal, to come and keep house for him.

Along with Frau Raubal came her daughter, also named Angela, or Geli for short. Geli was a lively girl with a happy personality. With her crown of beautiful blond hair, she was just the sort of Aryan beauty Hitler craved. With Geli the future dictator had the only love affair of his life. It ended in tragedy.

At first Hitler regarded the blond girl as little more than a child. He took her on trips and showed her the beauty of the Bavarian countryside. She, in turn, did typing for her "Uncle Alf" and helped him in his political work.

Several years later, as Hitler's income increased, he moved to a large, expensive apartment on the Outer Prinz Regenten Strasse in Munich. There he brought the two Angelas, his half sister and his niece. Geli wanted a career as a singer and expected her devoted Uncle Alf to help her in her ambition.

By 1929 people began to suspect that Hitler had become more than a guardian of his pretty niece and that he was her lover. But to Hitler, love was one-sided. It meant that Geli must be his devoted slave and ask no questions. Though they were not married, he forbade her to see other men. At the same time he reserved the right to see any woman he wanted to see.

There were many lovers' quarrels between Hitler and his niece. It was always Geli who had to give in. If she complained, Hitler would curse her and lock her in the apartment.

After some months of this, Geli began to tire of her uncle's conduct. He was too much the tyrant. Being a girl of some independence, she tried to meet other men. Finally she decided that there was no future for her in Munich. She would give up her home with her uncle and go to Vienna.

When Hitler heard the news he went into a violent rage. Geli would do as she was told. She would not go to Vienna or anywhere else without his permission.

One day, just as Hitler was getting into his car about to go to a political meeting, Geli called down to him from a window of their apartment in Munich, "Then you won't let me go to Vienna?"

"No!" Hitler shouted from his car. That was final.

Very little is known about what happened after that. Geli went to her mother's home in Berchtesgaden. There she was seen walking around the house with a little box holding a dead canary.

The next morning, September 18, 1931, Geli Raubal was found dead, with a bullet in her heart. She was just 23 years old.

Hitler was shattered. He wept bitterly for days. He knelt at Geli's grave. His friends even thought that he might kill himself in remorse.

No one knows how or why Geli died. There were all sorts of rumors. Some said that Geli had committed suicide, others that Hitler had driven her insane, or that he had her killed because he was afraid she would tell the press about their affair. Some even claimed the Nazis had murdered her so that a woman would not turn Hitler from his mission as Germany's savior.

No one knows. All that is certain is that the man with but little love in his life began to hate more and more.

Hitler Drives to Power

"I REGARD the present German Reich as neither a democracy nor a republic, but a Marxist-Jewish international pigsty."

This is the way Adolf Hitler described the Weimar Republic, set up in Germany in 1919 just after the end
of World War I. He said that this government was a
child of defeat, and he had only contempt for it.

What was the Weimar Republic? It was a democratic
state. It had a President who served for seven years, and
a Chancellor who headed the Cabinet. In the German
parliament there were two houses, the *Reichsrat,* which
was something like the United States Senate, and the
Reichstag, which resembled the House of Representa-
tives. But the Germans at that time had more than twenty-five political parties. This meant that elections had to
be held often because no one party was strong enough
to get a workable majority in the *Reichstag.* None of
the elections helped to break the deadlock.

In spite of this weakness, the Weimar Republic was
a state in the Western tradition. For many years the
Germans had been under the autocratic rule of the
Hohenzollern family and there had been little democracy
in the Empire. Now, after World War I, an attempt was
being made inside Germany to give the German people
a republic and a democratic way of life.

To Hitler, the belief in democracy, the faith that
people could and should rule themselves, was simply

what he called "crazy brains." He was convinced that they needed a good, strong leader—preferably himself.

Hitler and his followers were not the only ones who scorned the Weimar Republic. The Communists hated it, too. But Nazis and Communists hated each other with equal fervor. In the 1920's Hitler's Nazis engaged in a street battle with the Communists. The two rival parties beat each other with fists, pistols, and rifles. Many were killed on both sides. It was a bloody, sickening business, this battle of the street bullies.

In the *Reichstag* elections of 1928, the Nazis won only 12 seats, while the Communists had 54. But two years later, in the election of 1930, Hitler won an amazing victory. The strength of the Nazi Party suddenly rose to 107 deputies in the *Reichstag*. The number of Communist deputies went to 77.

Hitler's drum-beating tactics had been successful. This time he had succeeded in getting behind him a mass of citizens who had never taken the trouble to vote.

Two more years of political battle lay ahead. In July, 1932, the Nazis won 230 seats in the *Reichstag*. They were now the largest single political party in Germany, but Hitler was still short a majority because there were so many different parties. Still determined to achieve power only by legal means, he redoubled his efforts to win supporters for his side.

In the elections of November, 1932, Hitler received a setback. The Nazis, though still out in front, lost some ground. The number of Nazi deputies in the *Reichstag* dropped to 196. Meanwhile, the Communist strength rose to one hundred seats.

This meant a deadly battle between the Brown Fascist and the Red Communist parties. Both the Nazis on the right and the Communists on the left wanted to be ready to take over political power.

The loss of seats in the November, 1932, election worried Hitler greatly. Was his moment passing? Were the German people turning away from him?

Now he found help where he least expected it.

At that time there were others besides the Nazis and Communists in Germany who had no use for the Weimar Republic. Among them were the monarchists, who

wanted the Hohenzollern family to come back to rule
Germany, and army officers who felt they had lost caste
in the republic. There were also the Junker landowners
on their big estates, and the barons of heavy industry and
finance, who were frightened lest the Communists come
to power and take their property away from them.

All of these people began to believe that Adolf Hitler
and his Nazis could be useful to them. Granted, the
Nazis were crude, nasty, even vicious. Still, they would
be the rocks against which the growing wave of revolution might be shattered. "Let us give them a chance at
power," these people said. "If they do not behave, we
will throw them out."

Soon money began to flow to Hitler and the Nazis
from those threatened interests. The Junkers and the industrialists believed they could control this strange leader
who, they hoped, would help them keep their power over
the masses. They were not disturbed by Hitler's anti-
capitalist program. They believed it was only a trick to
get the attention of the people.

Little did they know the true nature of the man they
had decided to support. They had grabbed a dragon by
the tail.

By 1932 Hitler had decided that he wanted to be either
president or chancellor of Germany. Once he was secure in one of these offices, he would run the country
in his own way.

On April 10 of that year, Hitler ran for president
against General Paul von Hindenburg, the great German
hero of World War I. Von Hindenburg was re-elected
by 19,359,635 votes against Hitler's 13,418,051 votes.

Hitler was a poor loser. With typical bad taste he
attacked the old Prussian war lord. "He is eighty-five
years old," he said. "I am forty-five. I can wait."

This did not please either von Hindenburg or the
German people. The Junkers, the army officers, and the
industrialists, however, continued to believe that Hitler
was the one man who could best serve their interests
in an increasingly chaotic Germany.

Since 1930, a series of chancellors had governed Germany under emergency powers. On May 29, 1932, the
moderate Chancellor Heinrich Brüning was dismissed

from office by von Hindenburg. A bitter political battle
began behind the scenes. Three groups joined together
to seize power—the Junkers from the East, the West
German industrialists, and the officers of the *Reichswehr,*
the national army.

These three groups took over the cabinet. They were
first headed by Franz von Papen, a shrewd politician and
master of intrigue who was called "the devil in top hat,"
and then by General Kurt von Schleicher, an army man.
Von Papen and von Schleicher began to fight each other.
Von Schleicher wanted a military dictatorship. President
von Hindenburg, even though he was a former general,
was afraid of this because he felt it might mean civil
war.

We have seen that important people in the three top
level groups of Germany were already supporting Hitler
because he was the deadly enemy of the Communists,
whom he wanted to destroy. Now, the wily von Papen
paid a visit to the aged President von Hindenburg.

Hitler, said von Papen, could be trusted to form a
government. True, he was rough, unpolished, loud. But
he had great support in Germany and many millions of
Germans believed in him. Von Papen was sure that
Hitler would place in his cabinet a number of conserva-
tive men who would hold the fiery Nazi in line. Unless
Hitler was named chancellor, said von Papen, there was
a good chance that the country would fall into civil war.

The old President did not know what to do. He had
little use for this crude Hitler, this upstart lance corporal of the war.

Then two other important persons came to the aid of
von Papen. Both Oskar von Hindenburg, the president's
son, who was deeply worried about his estate in the East,
and a rich banker of Cologne named Baron Kurt von
Schroeder, told the President that von Papen was right.
Hitler had to be made chancellor.

At last the old man relented, but with great reluc-
tance. On January 30, 1933, he named Hitler chancellor
of Germany.

It was a great moment for the little man who had
once been an unwashed tramp on the streets of Vienna.
Far into the night, singing Nazis with flaming torches

marched by the window of the chancellery to cheer him. He was Chancellor of Germany! And he had kept his promise. There had been no *putsch*, no revolution. Everything was constitutional and legal.

The vast majority of the German people were unaware of it at the time, but the Weimar Republic had just committed suicide without knowing it. The Germans were plunging rapidly into their twentieth century Dark Age.

Why the Germans Accepted Hitler

How was it possible for Adolf Hitler and his gang of assorted misfits, thugs, and murderers to take over control of a great civilized nation?

Hitler was a product of his times. After the defeat of Germany and the Central Powers in World War I, the political situation was chaotic. Hitler and his Nazis were an answer to a people miserable in defeat, longing for a new self-respect, determined to come back after losing the war.

The depression of 1929 hit Germany hard. There were millions out of work, millions barely kept alive by the dole. The average German could not count on holding the job he had. He had no idea how long he would be able to provide food and a roof for himself and his family. He was anxious to put an end to hard times by "decisive" action of some kind.

Then along came Hitler. All his speeches could be reduced to a single, simple formula for hope: "Come to me. I will lead you to a glorious future. I will cure your problems, all of them, from unemployment on."

It was a deadly effective siren song. The unhappy Germans listened, took leave of reason, and fell into the trap.

Why did the Germans accept Hitler?

There is no easy answer. The explanation lies in the very nature of German culture. Over the course of the last two centuries the German people, like all other peoples,

have developed a "national character." This character
has been shaped in the family and in the schoolroom. It
is by no means inborn, and it does not mean the same
thing as "racial character." The traits that have been developed in the German people are obedience, thorough-
ness, love for discipline and order, respect for the State
rather than for the individual, subservience to the
"leader."

For generations the Germans have been taught that
it is most important to do exactly what the leader wants
them to do. This may be fine in a democratic state where,
if the leader shows himself to be weak or sinister, he
can be voted out of office. But in Germany the people followed even an evil genius like Hitler simply because they
were trained to follow the leader—no matter what he
did.

The Germans, actually, were caught between East and
West. In the West, people stress the ideas of the eight-
eenth century Age of Reason—liberty, equality, frater-
nity, democracy, liberalism, constitutionalism, parliamen-
tarianism, tolerance. In the East, people were conditioned
to accept authoritarianism, dictatorship, worship of the
State, do-what-you're-told. The Germans were in the
middle. They desperately wanted to accept the high ideals
of the West, but they were too deeply indoctrinated with
the harsh philosophy of the East.

The following paragraphs, written by a British historian,
A. J. P. Taylor, help to explain the reasons for the initial
successes of Hitler and his Nazis.

"The history of the Germans is a history of extremes.
It contains everything except moderation, and in the
course of a thousand years the Germans have experienced
everything except normality. They have dominated Europe, and they have been the helpless victims of the domination of others; they have enjoyed liberties unparalleled
in Europe, and they have fallen victims to despotisms
equally without parallel; they have produced the most
transcendental philosophers, the most spiritual musi-
cians, and the most ruthless and unscrupulous politicians.
A *German* has meant at one moment a being so senti-
mental, so trusting so pious, as to be too glad for this
world; and at another a being so brutal, so unprincipled,

so degraded, as to be not fit to live. Both descriptions are true; both types of Germans have existed not only at the same epoch, but in the same person.

"Only the normal person, not particularly good, not particularly bad, healthy, sane, moderate—he has never set his stamp on German history. Geographically the people of the center, the Germans have never found a middle way of life, either in their thoughts or least of all in their politics. One looks in vain in their history for a *juste milieu,* for common sense—the two qualities which have distinguished France and England. Nothing is normal in German history except violent oscillations." [1]

There are two different points of view on the subject of German guilt for Hitler and the Nazis. One view has it that the Germans invited the Nazi tyranny upon themselves. It was all done legally. And then, it is said, when they saw the nature of the evil of Nazism, they did not have the courage to throw it out.

The same point of view holds that, now that the Germans have recovered from the debacle of World War II and are among the most prosperous people in the world today, they want to forget all about Hitler and the Nazis. But they cannot escape blame. This view says that too many Germans freely supported Hitler, and many others who were not Nazis approved his major policies because they believed he would make Germany strong.

A second point of view holds that it is unfair to blame *all* the German people for the excesses of the Hitler regime. This view has it that millions of "decent Germans" were trapped by Hitler and his henchmen, and there was little they could do about it. Above all, it is said, it is unwise to blame the new German generation of young people for the sins of their elders.

As always, there are elements of truth on both sides of this argument. But on the basic facts historians do not differ:

1. The Germans were politically weak even before Hitler.

2. Hitler exploited the beliefs and fears of a frustrated

---

[1] A. J. P. Taylor, *The Course of German History* (New York, 1946), p.1.

people. His clear purpose was to destroy European civilization and replace it with a barbarian empire.

3. The Germans accepted him as the Messiah for whom they were awaiting.

4. This political monster brought disaster and ruin both to Germany and the world.

The Burning of the "Reichstag"

IT WAS 9 P.M. on the evening of February 17, 1933, when word spread through Berlin: "The *Reichstag* is on fire!

It was not a joke. Flames were rising over the cupola of the great building where Germany's laws were made. Before long the entire building was in ruins.

Within a few minutes of the alarm, screaming sirens announced the arrival of Hitler on the scene. Word of the fire had reached him while he was dining at Dr. Joseph Goebbels' house. The Nazi *Fuehrer* put on a show of terrible anger. The fire was set by the Communists, he shouted. It was a "sign from Heaven." The Nazi fist would smash these traitors down!

At the *Reichstag* the police arrested a suspect, a weakminded, 24-year-old Dutch vagabond named Marinus van der Lubbe, who had once belonged to a Communist club in Holland. According to the police, van der Lubbe had set fire to the building in twenty-three different places, using firelighters, cloths, towels, and curtains. They said that he took a zigzag course through the flames, even though he came out untouched by fire. Van der Lubbe did not fight back nor did he try to escape.

The next day the police arrested Ernst Torgler, leader of the Communists in the *Reichstag;* Georgi Dimitrov, a prominent Bulgarian Communist; and two other Bulgarian Communists, Vassili Tanev and Simon Popov.

Before the ashes of the *Reichstag* were cold, the Nazi

press, at Hitler's orders, shouted loudly that the murderous Communists had been stopped just in time. The fire, it said, was a signal for the beginning of a Communist campaign of terror.

Hitler shouted that he would destroy the Communists. He would hang the suspects at once, without trial, in front of the *Reichstag* so that the people could see how Nazis wiped out these "sub-human vermin."

But people all over the world felt that there was something most unusual about this fire. From everywhere came demands that the so-called plotters be given a fair trial. So great was the clamor that the Nazis could not ignore it. They had to bring the accused to court.

It was an amazing trial. The center of attention was the Dutch vagrant, van der Lubbe. He appeared to have collapsed completely. He sat by the hour with his head bowed. His eyes were unseeing—he took no notice of those around him. For days at a time he was so stupefied that he could not wipe his own nose. His lawyer did it for him, using paper handkerchiefs.

The Bulgarian, Dimitrov, proved to be a most difficult witness. Storming and ranting at his accusers, he showed the falsity of the charges against him. He was obviously innocent, and he took advantage of his position in the center of the limelight to put on a good show.

Hitler stayed away from the courtroom, possibly because he felt himself too big for this business. But there was a dramatic duel when Dimitrov and Goering came face to face in the courtroom.

"You are very afraid of my questions, are you not, Herr Minister?" Dimitrov asked.

Goering exploded: "I am not afraid of you, you crook! You belong to the gallows! Wait until I get you outside the power of this court!"

Then something most unexpected happened. The four Communists were found innocent. In spite of the most careful preparations, the case against them was not proved. Hitler had no choice but to let them go.

Only the pathetic, obviously mad van der Lubbe, who had said again and again that he alone started the fire, was found guilty. He was condemned to death and beheaded by hand ax in the courtyard of Leipzig prison.

The execution was pitiful. Not until the last minute did van der Lubbe believe that all this was in earnest. He must have had some kind of previous agreement with the Nazis. He probably thought that the trail was a Nazi show, and that he would go free.

Van der Lubbe's eyes opened wide with fright and horror when he at last realized that he was about to die. He shrieked and cried and had to be dragged, step by step, to the scaffold. The screams went on until the moment the ax came down. He was trying to say someting like, "Let me speak! Not alone! Not alone!"

Soon the real story of the burning of the *Reichstag* came out. *The Nazis had set the fire themselves and blamed it on the Communists!*

What had happened was this. Hitler had been in power for a month, and needed a big propaganda victory for the elections that were to take place the next week. Dr. Goebbels had a beautiful Nazi idea. Why not burn down the *Reichstag*, that awful symbol of German democracy, and then blame it on Hitler's enemies?

And that was it. A group of ten storm troopers entered the *Reichstag* building by way of a tunnel that ran from Goering's quarters. They prepared the fire by soaking curtains and rugs with inflammable liquids. Meanwhile, van der Lubbe, a pyromaniac, was encouraged to start some small fires of his own. Thus, the dupe van der Lubbe merely helped the Nazis to get the blaze going without realizing that he alone could never have done so much damage. It was Goering who set the police on his trail.

The *Reichstag* fire served Hitler well. It achieved exactly what he had hoped for—the end of the German Republic. It not only changed the imposing *Reichstag* building into a hollow shell, but it also gave Hitler a legitimate reason to crush his opponents.

The day after the fire Hitler proclaimed a "national emergency." He suspended such civil rights as freedom of speech, press, and assembly. Pacifists, liberals, democrats, and socialists were ruined, along with a million marks worth of glass and masonry.

Millions of Germans believed the charge that the *Reichstag* fire was to be a signal for a Communist revolt. In the elections of March 5, 1933, the Nazis increased their number of deputies in the *Reichstag* from 196 to 288, their popular vote from 11,737,000 to 17,277,200. This was only 44 per cent of the total votes, but along with the Nationalist Party it was enough to give Hitler 52 per cent of the total votes.

Hitler now had the power he wanted. The first act of his new *Reichstag* was to bury itself and the constitution. By an Enabling Act, they turned over the power for making laws to Hitler alone.

Thus the Germany of the Weimar Republic went up in flames, and from its smoke rose the Nazi Third Reich.

The word "Reich" means empire. The First Reich was the Holy Roman Empire (800-1806). The Second Reich was the Empire founded by Otto von Bismarck (1871-1918). The Third Reich, said Hitler, would be the greatest of all. It would last for a thousand years, he said.

The Blood Purge of June 30, 1934

ERNST RÖHM was a hard, stocky, little man who had been wounded three times in World War I. Half his nose was shot away, his cheek scarred by a bullet wound. A professional soldier, a freebooter, he was always looking for a fight. "Since I am a bad man," he was fond of saying, "war appeals to me more than peace."

It was Röhm who took the German Workers' Party, a small club of German workers, and made it into the National Socialist German Workers' Party, which, under Hitler, became the Nazi Party. He also built up the S.A., the brown-shirted storm troopers who fought and won the battle of the streets against the Communists. Without Röhm's "Brown Popular Army" Hitler would never have come to power.

Adolf Hitler and Ernst Röhm were close friends for fifteen years. The *Fuehrer* told Röhm that he would never forget the fine work he had done for the Nazi movement. "I want to thank Heaven," Hitler said, "for having given me the right to call a man like you my friend and comrade-in-arms."

Röhm wanted his S.A. storm troopers taken into the *Reichswehr*, but the proud officers of the army would not hear of it. What? Make these misfits and roughnecks, these chicken farmers, hotel porters, and thieves, officers in the great German army? Never!

Röhm wanted even more. He did not like the way things were going. The Nazi revolution, he said, had started out as a real revolution, but it had slowed down. "The National Socialist struggle," Röhm said, "has been a Socialist revolution. It has been the revolution of a workers' movement. Those who made this revolution must also be the ones to speak for it."

What Röhm was saying was this: Hitler's revolution was pulling in two directions. The very name of the party— National Socialist—spelled trouble. It was a combination of two movements—nationalism and socialism. The difficulty was that Socialism was *international*. How could one have "National Internationalism?" It just did not make sense. But a great deal about Nazism made no sense.

Röhm and other Nazi leaders such as Gregor Strasser felt that a second revolution was necessary. The Party, they said, must proceed along the road to socialism. And only the S.A. could bring about that second revolution. Even Dr. Goebbels, the propaganda chief, and Heinrich Himmler, head of the S.S. elite troops, seemed to share this point of view.

But Hitler knew that the real power in Germany was the *Reichswehr*, the regular army, not the S.A. He was certain that he could hold power only with the help of the *Reichswehr*, and he was not willing to oppose its officers.

Hitler tried to reason with Röhm. "Forget the idea of a second revolution," he said. "Believe in me. Don't cause us any trouble."

But Röhm, a stubborn man, would not listen. Nobody, he said, was going to break up his brown army, not even Hitler. It was a dangerous way to treat a man who was well on the way to becoming Germany's dictator.

The more he thought about it, the surer Hitler was that Röhm was dangerous to the Nazi cause. If Hitler was to become the real chief of the German Reich he would have to get rid of Röhm and his friends. They simply would not listen to reason.

Goebbels and Himmler, well aware of the power and determination of the *Fuehrer*, decided to jump on the Hitler bandwagon. Never again would they call for a "second revolution." Never again would they even dream of opposing the *Fuehrer* on anything. A deciding element in their decision may have been that Hermann Goering, head of the *Gestapo,* the relentless secret police, was loyal to Hitler.

Hitler decided that he would show no mercy to those who dared oppose his will. He flew down to Wiessee in Upper Bavaria, where Röhm was staying at the Hanslbauer sanitorium, a kind of private hotel. Röhm lay in bed, deep asleep. Hitler entered the room quietly, awakened Röhm, and arrested him.

Röhm, still unbelieving, was clapped into prison. He was given a gun and told that Hitler wanted him to take his own life within ten minutes.

Röhm could scarcely believe it. He refused to use the gun. "Adolf himself should do the dirty work," he said.

Ten minutes went by. Then the door to the cell opened, and from outside there poured a stream of bullets. Röhm died under the fire.

Meanwhile, one hundred and fifty top S.A. leaders had been arrested by Goering in Berlin and placed in a coal cellar at the Cadet School at Lichterfelde. Most of these doomed men had no idea that they were to be shot by Hitler's orders. In fact, many of them went to their deaths shouting, *"Heil* Hitler!"

It was a hideous massacre. The victims, four at a time, were led out to a wall in the courtyard. Then an S.S. man opened their shirts and drew a black circle, with a piece of charcoal, around the left part of the chest. This was the target. A few yards from the wall was a firing squad of eight men with rifles.

An officer shouted: "The *Fuehrer* wills it. *Heil Hitler!* Fire!"

On it went, hour after hour. The firing squads had to be changed frequently, for the men doing the killing could not stand the strain for very long. After a while their shots would miss the charcoal-drawn target, and the victims, still living, would lie screaming and writhing on the ground. Then an officer would finish them off with a shot to the head.

From time to time the bodies were taken away in a butcher's tin-lined truck.

No one knows how many were killed in that terrible blood purge of June 30, 1934. There were victims in many other German cities, but not all were executed.

Some Nazi chiefs who remained loyal to Hitler took advantage of the day's chaos to get rid of their own enemies. Goering sent six assassins to kill former Chancellor Kurt von Schleicher in his villa. The assassins also murdered von Schleicher's wife. Gregor Strasser, like Röhm, was killed in his cell. Both von Schleicher and Gregor Strasser had been bitter enemies of Goering.

Hundreds died in the blood-bath. In Munich, the 73-year-old Gustav von Kahr, who eleven years before had crushed Hilter's beer hall *putsch,* was dragged from his home. A few days later his corpse, badly battered, was found in a swamp. Hitler, or one of his men, had not forgotten.

There were some horrible mistakes. Willy Schmidt, a well-known music critic, was killed. He was confused with another Willy Schmidt who was being sought by the murderers!

"In those hours," Hitler said, "I was the supreme judge of the German people."

On this gruesome pile of corpses Adolf Hitler made his way to supreme power. When the carnage was over, Adolf Hitler was master not only of his own Party but also of all Germany. No one dared to challenge him.

"There won't be another revolution in Germany," Hitler boasted.

CHAPTER FOURTEEN 卐卐卐卐卐卐卐卐卐卐卐

A Man Possessed

WHAT kind of man was this who changed the course of history?

Hitler never stood out in a crowd until he began to talk. He was a medium-sized man, flabby, stooping, with nondescript brown hair and blue eyes. There was something almost feminine about him, about the way he carried himself, about the way he walked. His shoulders were narrow, his hips wide.

His face was pale, and he appeared to be sickly. According to Mussolini, Hitler sometimes used rouge on his cheeks to hide an unhealthy pallor. He had a small mustache and a strand of unruly hair that fluttered across his brow. But there was a curious power in his eyes, a sort of hypnotic quality that fascinated millions of Germans. "Can't you feel the terrific power of his personality?" the Nazi Foreign Minister Joachim von Ribbentrop asked a doctor at Nuremberg. "Can't you see how he swept people off their feet? I don't know if you can, but we can feel it. It is overwhelming!"

It is not easy to understand Hitler's mind without help from the psychologist (the scholar who studies human behavior) and the psychiatrist (the doctor who studies the human mind). One thing is certain—Hitler was not a normal man. His hysterical tantrums, his feeling that people were always working against him, his hatreds, his alternate periods of joy and gloom, all these symptoms are familiar to the psychiatrist.

50

The Bristish historian, H. R. Trevor-Roper, described Hitler's mind in a remarkable sentence: "A terrible phenomenon, imposing indeed in its granite harshness and yet infinitely squalid . . . like some huge barbarian monolith, the expression of giant strength and savage genius, surrounded by a festering heap of refuse—old tins and dead vermin, ashes and eggshells."

Professor Max Huber, a German anthropologist, called before the Munich court of justice in 1924 to present evidence of Hitler's mental instability, said, "Hitler has a low, sloping forehead, an ugly nose, wide cheekbones, and small eyes. The expression of his face reveals an individual who has no proper control over himself and is mentally unstable."

There were two sides to Hitler's character, so different that he seemed to be two entirely different men. At one moment he could be charming and friendly. He loved music and he liked to play with children. He could talk calmly with his friends about the beauties of nature.

Then suddenly, at mention of one of his enemies, he would go into a rage and lose control of himself. His face would turn red and swell with fury. He would scream at the top of his voice, spit out curses, wave his arms through the air, and smash his hands on the table. Sometimes he would even foam at the mouth, drop to the floor, and begin chewing the carpet in rage. This is why some Germans called him *"Der Teppichfresser,"* "that carpet-chewer."

Then, as quickly as he had begun, he would turn off the tantrum and start talking quietly as if nothing had happened. It was very sick behavior.

Hitler was a good actor and knew how to exploit his rages. At times he put on a show to get what he wanted, especially when he wished to shock or frighten an opponent. He did this in his interviews with Chancellor Kurt von Schuschnigg before he snatched Austria, and with President Emil Hácha before he took over Czechoslovakia.

Hitler was a fanatical egoist. He began to think of himself as a man of destiny, as a German Messiah. He believed that he was infallible—that he could make no mistakes. He refused to admit that he was wrong at any time.

He declined to give any other person any credit for his ideas.

When half of Europe lay at his feet, Hilter's egoism changed to megalomania—a disordered mental condition in which a person has grandiose delusions. By this time he believed that he was the greatest German who ever lived, a kind of half-god.

He had no real friends. He mistrusted everyone. There were only two or three people with whom he was on close enough terms to use the German *"Du,"* the familiar form of address among friends. Von Ribbentrop said after the war: "I don't think anybody really ever had a heart-to-heart talk with him as man to man. Not a single one. . . . I don't think he ever really bared his heart to anyone."

Hitler was a lone wolf. It was always that way, even during the early days before he came to power. When he was a young politician striving for power, he would be invited to the homes of rich people curious to meet him. The story is told that on one such visit, on a Sunday afternoon in 1921, he arrived in his dirty trench coat and sat quietly and awkwardly for an hour or so. But when someone mentioned the Treaty of Versailles, he suddenly forgot his loneliness, sprang to his feet, and launched into an impassioned tirade.

Hitler hated "experts." From his early years on he despised those who had more learning than he. His library was filled with beautifully bound books, but he read few of them. Action, emotion, and will ruled his life—intelligence never. He wanted to be a doer, not a scholar.

"I have the gift," he once said, "of reducing all problems to their most simple foundations."

Hitler loathed work of any kind. He was a lazy man who wanted to be left alone to dream his big dreams. Paper work, which bored him, he left to his assistants. He still believed that he was an artist—a potentially great architect or painter—who had been called by destiny to serve Germany. He wanted to rebuild Berlin and Munich, with huge buildings, like the Pyramids, reflecting the greatness of Germany's rulers.

In many ways Hitler led a Spartan life. He did not smoke, and no one dared to smoke in his presence. He drank no alcohol. He avoided tea and coffee. He never touched meat. He was perfectly happy with a plate of scrambled eggs, provided that the dish was tested for poison beforehand. He liked to munch on candy and cream buns.

He was so nervous that he found it almost impossible to sleep. Often he would wake up in the middle of the night and walk restlessly. Sometimes he would shout for help. Shaking with fear, he would gasp as though suffocating. One of his servants told how once, in the early hours of the morning, Hitler was found swaying in the middle of the room and crying, "He! He! He's been here!" His lips were blue. His fists were clenched. Perspiration rolled down his face. Suddenly he began to speak in broken phrases, using words that made no sense at all. "Who's that in the corner?" he demanded.

Hitler loved the music of Richard Wagner. In fact, the only master he ever recognized was this composer who thrilled him with his great, mystical Teutonic operas. He —Hitler—would bring Wagnerian ideas to life.

Hitler pictured himself as Siegfried fighting the dragon. He was Frederick the Great, who smashed down the enemies of Prussia. He was the crusader who would slay the Bolshevik monster. He was the mystic who conducted ceremonies on a mountaintop to the everlasting glory of those who had fallen in his struggle for power.

Yet, Adolf Hitler was not a German. It has been pointed out that it was his very un-German qualities that appealed most to the German people. For example, Hitler hated meat, alcohol, and exercise, precisely those things which the solid German burghers liked most. Thus, it is said, the German people, who were a little ashamed of their vices, turned to this ascetic little man who seemed to have all the virtues. Hitler was the savior who would lead them to salvation, happiness, and prosperity.

Hitler liked the company of beautiful women, but he was careful to avoid marriage. He felt that being tied to one woman would hurt his political career. To him, his career came first.

Among the women in Hitler's life, after Geli Raubal, was Frau Hélène Bechstein, of the famous piano manufacturing family, who introduced him to society and helped raise funds for the Nazi Party in its early days. Frau Winnifried Wagner, daughter of the composer Richard Wagner, was his great and admiring friend, and there were others: Leni Riefenstahl, who directed motion pictures of the Nuremberg rallies and the Olympic Games in Berlin in 1936; Unity Mitford, an eccentric Englishwoman who tried to end her life because of her love for Hitler; and Eva Braun, who became his wife a day before both died in a suicide pact.

But there was never a Josephine or a Madame Pompadour in Hitler's life. He liked to talk to women, but they had to keep their place—outside of men's business.

German women played a most important role in Hitler's drive to power. Millions were entranced by his hypnotic eyes. *"Der schoene Adolf,"* "The handsome Adolf," they called him.

Those who knew Hitler saw him in different ways. To some he was a greatly gifted political leader; to others he was a vicious madman.

After the war one of the German military leaders, General Franz Halder, commented: "While I was working with him I was always looking for signs of genius in him. I tried hard to be honest and impartial, and not to be blinded by my antipathy to the man. I *never* found genius in him, only the devil."

The French Ambassador to Germany from 1931–1938, M. A. François-Poncet, saw him this way: "Hitler was no normal being. He was rather a morbid personality, a quasi-madman, a character out of the pages of Dostoevski, a man possessed."

Portrait of a Hater

THE MOTIVATING force in Adolf Hitler's life was hate. As a child, he hated his father. Later, he directed his malice not only toward his real enemies, but against imagined ones. In the end, it was the hate fostered in his own heart that destroyed him.

As a young man, Hitler was fascinated by such instruments of death as revolvers, knives, and blackjacks. In his Munich days he carried a heavy riding whip made of hippopotamus hide.

In the days when he was striving for political power, Hitler decided to use his talent as an artist to help the Party. He designed a piece of false money on which he drew a man in an open shirt, holding in his right hand a sword dripping with blood. The left hand held the hair of a woman's severed head.

Mean and petty, spiteful and vindictive, Hitler had no sense of generosity. Pity and mercy to him were only signs of weakness. "There is no keener pleasure," he said, "than to haul a defeated rival under the knife."

Hitler had no sense of humor, only what the Germans call *Schadenfreude,* joy in the bad luck of other people. He would laugh with delight at movies showing old Jews being beaten or forced to scrub the streets. He enjoyed movies that showed his enemies being executed.

In 1937, visitors to the Exhibit of German Paintings in Munich were treated to the rare spectacle of the Chancellor of the German Reich tearing and cutting to pieces with his own hands some paintings that failed to please him.

But above all Hitler hated the Jews. This was the mainspring of his thoughts and actions, the most consistent passion of his life.

He also hated Frenchmen. "They are degenerate Negroes and they must be crushed!"

He hated Czechs. "They are Slavic swine."

He hated Russians. "They are uncouth, dirty, filthy mongrels."

Since his poverty-stricken Munich and Vienna days, Hitler had hated the comfortable middle-class world which, he believed, had failed to recognize his genius. His resentment against it was so great that he was determined someday to revenge himself against it, but his work as a politician was such that he had to make friends among the people he hated.

When Hitler appeared in society the effect was extraordinary. The German writer Konrad Heiden gives this description of Hitler's debut into society: "Wearing an elegant suit, he entered the room carrying an enormous bouquet of roses and kissed his hostess' hand. When the guests were introduced to him he looked like a public prosecutor assisting at the execution of a death sentence. When he began to speak, a baby started crying in one of the neighboring rooms; it had been awakened by his explosively loud and penetrating voice."

The more he hated, the lonelier he grew. By the last few months of his life his hatred had cut him off from contact with almost all human beings.

For the world, the most dangerous thing about this hate-inspired man was that he regarded war as good. "War," he said, "is the most natural, the most everyday matter. War is eternal. War is universal. War is life. Any struggle is war. War is the origin of all things."

Again, he said, "I want war. To me all means will be right. My motto is not 'Don't, whatever you do, annoy the enemy.' My motto is 'Destroy him by all and any means.' I am the one who will wage the war!"

CHAPTER SIXTEEN

The Anatomy of a Liar

ADOLF HITLER was not only a hater, he was one of the most consummate liars of all time. His disrespect for truth was equaled only by his disrespect for God and man. He had no moral sense whatever. All his life he practiced lying, cunning, and deceit in order to get what he wanted. It was his way to power, to war, and finally to death.

In his book, *Mein Kampf,* Hitler admitted his formula for success included the art of lying. "The masses of people," he wrote, "are not intelligent. Their understanding is feeble."

Hitler believed that the great mass of people had simple, primitive minds and were swayed chiefly by their emotions. Therefore, when one lied to the people, it was best to tell big lies. "They more readily fall victims to the big lie than the small lie, since they themselves often tell small lies in little matters, but would be ashamed to resort to large-scale falsehoods."

Another of Hitler's excuses for the big lie was, "The grossly impudent lie always leaves traces behind it, even when it is nailed down."

All the while he was preparing Germany for World War II, Hitler made speech after speech protesting his love of peace. "I was a common soldier in the war," he would shout. "I know what war is like. I would be insane if I ever wanted war again. Only our enemies want war."

Every time Hitler gobbled up a new piece of land in

Europe he would make a speech saying it was the last territory he wanted.

On August 22, 1939, Hitler called his highest army generals to a conference. He told them he intended to make a pact with Joseph Stalin, dictator of Soviet Russia, to attack and divide Poland. And then he added, "I shall give a good propaganda reason for starting the war, whether plausible or not. In starting and making war, it is not right, but victory, that matters."

"I am willing to sign anything," he said at one time. "I will do anything to further my policy. I am prepared to guarantee all frontiers and to make non-aggression pacts and friendly alliances with anybody. It would be sheer stupidity not to make use of such measures. . . . Why should I not make an agreement in good faith today and break it tomorrow if the future of the German people demands it?"

This was the man Konrad Heiden called "in a world of normalcy, a Nothing; in chaos, a Titan."

CHAPTER SEVENTEEN

Hitler the Orator 卐卐卐卐卐卐 卐卐卐 卐卐卐卐 卐

THE HUGE crowd in the Berlin *Sportpalast,* the Sports Palace, hums with expectancy. It is a cross section of the German public—grimy workers with gnarled hands, middle-class white-collar workers with protruding beer bellies and egglike heads, excited women, giggling girls, veterans of World War I, students with shining faces.

Suddenly the hall darkens and there is silence. A white spotlight fingers its way to the entrance in the rear of the hall. Then, to the blare of trumpets, the slight figure of Adolf Hitler appears. The spotlight follows him as he walks slowly up the aisle to the platform.

The crowd becomes hysterical at the sight of its Messiah. A dozen women faint. A loud, monotonous chant begins: *"Sieg Heil! Sieg Heil! Sieg Heil!"* "Hail to Victory!"

Hitler, bowing and smiling, stands before the crowd. He raises his hand, and the thunderous noise stops as though by magic.

The speaker's desk is specially rigged. In front of Hitler is a row of electrical buttons with which he can regulate the volume of sound, and the lighting. When he presses one button, the audience receives a go-ahead signal to applaud. When he presses another, there is silence. The whole scene is carefully stage-managed.

Hitler begins to speak in a slow, tenor voice. He attacks the Treaty of Versailles. He paints a sad picture of the misery of the German people. In a terribly solemn voice he tells his hearers what they must believe. He does not reason with them, he tells them!

His theme is simple. We Germans did not lose the war. We were stabbed in the back by Jews and Socialists. Down with the Communist pigs! Down with the international Socialists! Down with the international bankers! Down with Soviet Russia! Down with the Jews! Down with the democracies and their false promises! *Deutschland, erwache!* Germany, awake!

The crowd listens mostly in silence as Hitler begins to warm to his task. His voice mounts slowly. It grows hoarse and rasping, passionate.

"Why did England go to war against Germany in 1914?" shouts Hitler. "England went to war against us because of a great propaganda campaign in the press. And who was the chief of this commercial press? One man stands out— Northcliffe, a Jew!"

Lord Northcliffe, the British publisher, is not a Jew. But this makes no difference to the speaker.

"What reason did America have to go to war with Germany? When the war broke out, all the Jewish firms in the United States began to sell war materials. The corrupt American press, dependent on the stock exchange kings, began a great propaganda campaign. A huge pyramid of press lies was built up. And who set the tone for this agitation against Germany? The Hearst Press, a Jewish concern!"

William Randolph Hearst, the American publisher, was neither a Jew nor of Jewish descent. But again this made no difference to the speaker.

Now such words as "honor," "loyalty," "sacrifice," and "fatherland" come tumbling out of Hitler's gas-corroded throat. His right arm hacks the air as he drives his points home. He keeps brushing back his unruly lock of hair. He raves and he rants. The people in the audience take his words in deadly earnest. The emotional response to this "unknown soldier uttering the thoughts of millions" is tremendous. At this moment Adolf Hitler becomes the very symbol of the Germany that worships him.

Make no mistake about it. Here was the most effective orator of the mass age. Hitler knew well how to handle mobs of people. "The power brought about by great historical movements," he said, "always came through the magic of the spoken word."

The magic of the spoken word! None understood it better than he. His words made little or no sense. Frequently they were vulgar. This spellbinder was devoid of humor. His jokes were flat, stale.

Hitler's speeches were like dreams—chaotic, full of contradictions, and at times, meaningless. Many of his entranced listeners could never remember afterward just what he had said. All they knew was that he had started with gloomy words, with troubled and tragic phrases, but he had ended triumphantly. The Germans would awake from their long sleep and strike down their oppressors. Then the master German race would take its rightful, dominant place in the world.

This is the way one of Hitler's followers described his own feelings when he heard Hitler at a mass meeting in 1922: "His words were like a scourge. When he spoke of the disgrace of Germany, I was ready to spring on my enemy. . . . I looked around and saw that his magnetism was holding these thousands as one. . . . The intense will of the man, the passion of his sincerity, seemed to flow from him into me. I was exalted. It was just like a religion. . . . I gave him my soul."

CHAPTER EIGHTEEN

Knights of the Crooked Cross 卐卐 卐卐 卐卐 卐

AROUND Hitler there gathered a bizarre gang of misfits, fanatics, and ambitious politicians. All relied on Hitler to bring them either power, money, glory, or all three. They were a varied lot of scoundrels and murderers, midgets propelled into the seats of the mighty by the Nazi revolution.

In selecting his lieutenants, Hitler always asked himself these questions. Is he loyal to me? Is he a good Nazi? Once taken into the clan, will he devote his life to me and the Nazi cause?

Like the tyrants of past centuries, Hitler was shrewd enough to play off his comrades, the chief Nazis, one against the other. It was simple—they would hate each other so much that not one of them would ever get the chance to take Hitler's place.

There were dozens of these leading Nazis. Let us take a quick look at the life and work of some of them.

HERMANN WILHELM GOERING : NUMBER 2 NAZI

Hermann Wilhelm Goering was born on January 12, 1893, in Rosenheim, Bavaria, the son of a diplomat. He was a big, fat, wild man who loved women, beer, song, uniforms, and lion cubs in that order. Brought up to be a soldier, he began World War I as an infantry officer.

Later in the war Goering became a combat flyer. By 1918, he was the leader of a squadron of aviators that had been commanded by the famous Baron von Richthofen before his death. Captain Goering was an able, courageous flyer. He was decorated with the *Pour le Mérite,* one of the highest medals a German soldier could obtain in combat.

At the age of twenty-five, the happy-go-lucky Goering had everything a young man could want—fame, fortune, money. But with the ending of the war, his whole world crashed around him. Gone was the glory of army days. Suddenly he and thousands of other officers were out of work.

Goering's was the tragedy of the whole post-war generation, a generation of young men who knew little more than the business of killing. Goering became a transport pilot carrying passengers and mail between Denmark and Sweden. It was not glamorous work, but it was a living at least.

Worst of all, Goering's nerves began to fail him. He developed the habit of taking morphine.

Down on his luck, Goering went to Munich in 1921 to study economics. One night he heard Hitler speak at a small political meeting. Like many others, he was fascinated.

"I believe in this man," Goering said.

Soon the ex-captain and the ex-lance corporal were close friends. By the next year Goering had a job as leader of the newly formed Nazi Party army. During the whole Nazi drive for power, Goering was at Hitler's side.

Nearly everybody liked Goering, who had the poise and personal charm Hitler lacked. Goering was fond of good jokes, even those told at his own expense, and he enjoyed playing tricks on people. He laughed a lot. Germans fondly called him *"Unser Hermann,"* "Our Hermann."

The Germans liked to tell stories about Goering's love for uniforms of all kinds. The fat man often held great receptions and hunting parties at his vast estate, *Karinhall.* Here he would appear in fantastic uniforms that he had designed himself. One day it might be a sky-blue uniform, with which he carried an ivory-and-gold baton set with precious stones. On another day he would wear Bavarian leather shorts and a many-colored vest decorated with silver. Or he might wear a panther skin, as did the old Teutonic kings, with an elaborate headpiece crowned with horns. He even appeared, at times, in a brilliant white, flowing robe that might have been anything from a costume in a Wagnerian opera to the dress of a Venetian noble.

Goering reveled in his popularity. He told the latest funny stories about himself and laughed the loudest of anyone. He was always the good-humored fat man.

Goering was determined to let nothing stand in the way of the Nazi revolution. He so admired its leader, Hitler, that he even began to imitate him. This is from one of his talks (1936):

"Party comrades, friends! I have come to talk to you about Germany. *Germany must have a place in the sun!* We are rearming. Weak—we are at the mercy of the world.

"I must speak clearly. Some people are hard of hearing. They can only be made to listen if they hear the guns go off. We have no butter, my comrades. But I ask you— would you rather have butter or guns? Shall we import lard or metal parts? Let me tell you—to be prepared makes us powerful. Butter merely makes us fat!"

The audience roared with laughter. Goering was right. They wanted guns, not butter! But behind this seemingly good-natured, fat clown was the soul of a killer.

Goering was the creator of the *Gestapo,* from *Ge*heime *Sta*ats *Po*lizei. This was the dreaded secret police force that wiped out Hitler's enemies one by one inside Germany.

Goering started the first concentration camps in Germany, those evil prisons and slave-labor camps, which shocked the entire world. As head of the Four-Year Plan in 1936, he was responsible for creating the German war machine and making it ready for conflict. In World War II he commanded the *Luftwaffe,* the German air force.

At the Nuremberg trials of war criminals in 1945–1946 the court said that "Hermann Goering's guilt is unique in its enormity. The record discloses no excuse for this man."

Just an hour before he was to be hanged by order of the court, Goering took poison, which he had obtained somehow while in his cell. Many Germans, who remembered Goering with affection, thought this a good, if grim joke. "Our Hermann" fooled them once again!

RUDOLF HESS: NUMBER 3 NAZI

Rudolf Hess was a stiff, dark-haired, beetle-browed man with dark, staring eyes. He was born on April 26, 1896, in Alexandria, Egypt, of German parents. He was educated in Germany. In 1914, he volunteered for the army and joined the famous List Regiment, which had staggering losses. But Hess came out of the war alive, even though he was twice wounded.

Hess, the officer, met Hitler, the lance corporal, during the war. They met again in Munich after the war. Like Goering and many others, Hess was hypnotized by Hitler's fighting speeches. This was the man, Hess decided, who would save Germany from ruin.

From then on Hitler became Hess's idol. Hess followed Hitler through the Munich *putsch* in 1923 and was with him in Landsberg prison in 1924.

Hess was never far from his *Fuehrer's* side. Hitler tried out his speeches on the younger man, using him as a kind of sounding board. He often asked Hess, who had more polish than he, for advice on how to make the best impression on an audience.

As the Nazi movement gathered strength, Hess went higher and higher in the Party's councils. At the great rallies of the Nazi Party, Hess would introduce Hitler as if he were speaking of the Almighty. With humble devotion, with tears in his eyes, he would lead the crowd in hysterical *"Heils!"* to the *Fuehrer*.

"Mein Fuehrer," Hess would shout hoarsely, "our trust in you is unlimited! God protect the *Fuehrer!"*

Or again: "My *Fuehrer,* you are Germany! When you judge, the people judge!"

Hess's star rose with Hitler's, and in the service of his leader he acquired a long series of titles. He became Deputy *Fuehrer,* Leader of the Nazi Party, Member of the Secret Cabinet Council for Germany, Reich Minister without Portfolio, Member of the Ministerial Council for the Defense of the Reich. As deputy to Hitler he could make decisions in the name of his leader. He was at Hitler's side when the *Fuehrer* planned aggression against Austria, Czechoslovakia, and Poland.

After the war broke out in 1939, things changed. Hitler was busy with important military leaders, and the puppy-like, sensitive Hess was gradually pushed into the background. Hess fretted and fumed over his bad luck. Would it not be wonderful if he, Hess, would win back his beloved *Fuehrer* by a great act of sacrifice? It was a terrible tragedy, he thought, for Germans and British, blood brothers, Aryans all, to fight one another. He would fly alone to England, make peace with the British, and get them to join Germany in the coming war against the Soviet Union.

On May 10, 1941, just a month and a half before Hitler turned on his ally, Soviet Russia, Hess flew alone in a *Messerschmitt* fighting plane to Scotland. It was a fine piece of navigation. He crashed his plane, landed by parachute, and was captured by a farmer with a pitchfork. The British paid no attention to his pleas and put him in jail.

It was the end of a beautiful friendship. Hitler was enraged. Why had Hess done such a stupid thing? Who had asked him to be an angel of peace? The *Fuehrer* told the press that Hess had gone crazy.

"It seemed that Party Member Hess's mind was wandering," he said, "as a result of which he felt he would bring about an understanding between England and Germany. . . . The National Socialist Party regrets this idealist fell a victim to his insane idea. This, however, will have no effect on carrying on the war that has been forced on Germany."

Winston Churchill, British Prime Minister during World War II, had this to say about Hess: "Whatever may be the moral guilt of a German who stood near to Hitler, Hess has, in my view, atoned for this by his completely devoted and frantic deed of lunatic benevolence. He came to us of his own free will, and, though without authority, had something of the quality of an envoy. He was a medical and not a criminal case, and should be so regarded."

THE LITTLE MOUSE DOCTOR: PAUL JOSEPH GOEBBELS

Paul Joseph Goebbels was a thin, nervous, little man. He was, indeed, so tiny, he was almost a dwarf. As a young man he had been excessively bitter because he had a crippled foot.

Goebbels was born on October 29, 1897, in Rheydt, a little town in the Rhineland. He was seventeen at the outbreak of World War I, but he saw no service because of his handicap. Realizing that his body was too frail to bring him distinction, he decided to train his mind. He studied history, literature, and philosophy at six universities. He lived on a scholarship given him by a Catholic society. At Heidelberg, where he earned the degree of Doctor of Philosophy, he studied with a famous Jewish professor, Friedrich Gundolf, who taught him to revere Goethe and Shakespeare.

Goebbels at first attempted to publish novels and plays, but he had no success. Later, he turned to newspaper work. His first job was as editor of a Nazi newspaper in the Ruhr. He met Hitler, and the two men were immediately drawn to each other.

Goebbels' pen began to glorify his friend: "God gave Adolf Hitler the words to describe what is ailing Germany. You began at the bottom, as every truly great leader. And like every leader you grew even greater as your task grew greater. You became a wonder!"

Hitler loved this praise. And he was grateful to the ugly little man who so obviously worshiped him. In Goebbels he found someone who would listen to him for days. "A man who burns like a flame," he said of Goebbels.

Hitler also liked Goebbels' ideas and the way he expressed them. Goebbels believed, even though he had studied at universities, that "the intellect has poisoned our people." He said that intellectuals were "sickly people." With Hitler, he shared the conviction that people were swayed by their emotions, not by reason.

In 1926, Hitler made his young admirer a *Gauleiter,* or district leader, of the Berlin-Brandenburg group of the Nazi Party. "He will be responsible to me alone," said Hitler.

Thus a bond was forged that was not to be severed until both men were dead by their own hands.

People called Goebbels the little "Mouse-Doctor." When he came to Berlin, things began to hum. It was the old story of the country boy who came to the big city and showed the city slickers what was what. Goebbels kept himself in the limelight with his voice and his pen.

Goebbels was almost as good a speaker as Hitler. Hitler later said that Goebbels rose rapidly in the Nazi Party because he had "two qualities without which no one could master conditions in Berlin: intelligence and oratory."

Goebbels, like Hitler, knew how to stir up the masses by hammering away at simple points. He shouted, pleaded, cajoled, whispered, and screamed, all the while cutting the air with his right arm.

He was quick at inventing slogans too.

YOUR FATHERLAND IS CALLED GERMANY! LOVE IT ABOVE ALL! ACTION NOT WORDS!
GERMANY'S ENEMIES ARE YOUR ENEMIES. HATE THEM WITH YOUR WHOLE HEART!
HE WHO ABUSES GERMANY, ABUSES YOU AND YOUR DEAD. STRIKE YOUR FIST AGAINST HIM!
THE GERMAN ALWAYS BEFORE THE FOREIGNER AND JEW!
CERTAINLY THE JEW IS ALSO A MAN, BUT THE FLEA IS ALSO AN ANIMAL!
BELIEVE IN THE FUTURE! ONLY THEN CAN YOU BE A VICTOR!

Dr. Goebbels became Hitler's Minister for Popular Enlightenment and Propaganda. He had a flair for drama and pageantry, and was the man who ran Germany's artistic and literary life. He knew all about propaganda, publicity, advertising, promotion. He thought up tricks of which no one else would ever have dreamed. He would march at the head of a group of storm troopers, all of whom had white bands, colored with a red liquid, around their heads, so that they would be taken for "heroes" who had bled for the Party. He himself wore a kind of uniform which, together with his crippled foot, made people think he was a wounded war veteran.

Whenever Goebbels gave a talk at a mass meeting, he arrived late. As soon as the crowd became restless, he would stride to the platform amid a fanfare of trumpets. Against a background of uniforms and torchlights and Nazi eagles he would shout, "We Nazis know neither if nor but, *we demand* only either . . . or!

"*We demand* the restoration of German honor. Without honor there is no right to live.

"*We demand* for every working man work and bread! For the people, a place to live. No democrat has the right to deny these. We want action!

"*We demand* war against the profiteers, peace with the workers!

"*We demand* a solution to the Jewish question. We want all foreign races out of German life.

"*We demand* an end to the German parliament. We want a leader above the mob.

"*We demand* death sentences for crimes against the people! To the gallows with the profiteers and money-lenders!"

The little propaganda chief was, with Hitler, a top rabble-rouser of the Nazi revolution. Like Hitler, he was obsessed with the idea of Teutonic superiority. His racial fanaticism and violent anti-Semitism matched Hitler's. Both men hated the bourgeois world in which they lived, and both were ignorant of the world beyond Germany's frontiers. Both harbored hatreds, which, at times, reached the paranoiac (delusions of persecution).

When Hitler died, a suicide, in 1945, Goebbels refused to live any longer in a world that was not National Socialist. He killed himself. He remained loyal to Hitler to the very end.

HEINRICH HIMMLER: MASS MURDERER

He looked like a bland, harmless schoolteacher. But behind the narrow forehead, the pince-nez glasses, and the pleasant smile, was the most infamous mass murderer of all time.

Heinrich Himmler was born in Munich in 1900. He grew up in Landshut, where he attended the *Gymnasium*, or high school. He served in a Bavarian regiment during World War I, but never reached the front. After the war he studied at the *Technische Hochschule* in Munich, where he took his degree in agriculture. After joining the Nazi Party, he became a poultry farmer.

Unlike Goering and Goebbels, the roaring tigers of Naziland, Himmler was silent and fishlike. He had little to say. But in him Hitler saw a valuable servant, a loyal and efficient party comrade. Above all, Himmler was obedient to the master Nazi—he did as he was told. And, he was a man Hitler could trust.

Himmler organized and guided the S.S., the *Schutz-Staffel*, Hitler's black-shirted bodyguard. "It will be an elite of especially chosen men," said Himmler. He trained these men to be hard, arrogant, contemptuous. They were to be ready to kill Germans as well as foreigners. Their first duty was to protect the person of the *Fuehrer;* second, they were to spy inside and outside the Nazi Party.

So successful was Himmler as Reich leader of the S.S. that, in 1934, Hitler promoted him to the post of *Gestapo* chief. Himmler brought his most loyal S.S. men to work for the *Gestapo*. After studying other secret police systems, such as the *Ochrana* of Tsarist Russia and the *Cheka* and *G.P.U.* of Bolshevik Russia, Himmler made what he considered to be many improvements in the methods of the *Gestapo*.

Himmler's infamous reputation was due to his role as the master executioner of Nazi Germany. He was responsible for the deaths of millions of men, women, and children in the gas ovens of the Nazi concentration camps.

Himmler tried to escape at the end of World War II, but he was captured by the Allies. Knowing that he could not possibly survive a fair trial, he took poison and died almost instantly.

MURDERERS, THUGS, AND MOUNTEBANKS

The cast of characters in the Third Reich was sinister.

All revolutions seem to spew forth a band of human misfits who seize power, money, and glory for themselves, but the Nazis were a special collection. Here are a few more of the evil men who worked with Hitler:

—*Julius Streicher*, the number one Jew-baiter, sadist, thief, publisher of dirty literature. This squat, bald-headed, coarse little man was the editor of *Der Stuermer*, an anti-Semitic newspaper. Even Goering had a secret report on him: "Streicher likes to beat people with a riding whip, but only if he is in company with several persons helping him. Usually the beatings are carried out with sadistic brutality."

—*Fritz Sauckel*, bull-necked boss of millions of Nazi slave laborers. In a speech Sauckel declared that, "a great percentage of the foreign workers will remain in Germany even after victory to complete what the war has prevented us from finishing."

—*Alfred Rosenberg*, "intellectual leader" of the Nazi movement. Rosenberg led an art-looting staff which, during World War II, carried off to Germany 21,436 freight carloads of paintings, rare books, sculpture, and jewelry. Much of this found its way into the private collections of Reichsmarschall Hermann Goering.

—*Hans Frank*, brutal governor-general of Poland during World War II, and leader of the German Reign of Terror there. Frank had a program for killing every Pole except those needed as slaves for the German landlords in Poland. In his diary he wrote that "there are not enough forests in Poland to supply paper for the lists of Poles I have had killed."

—*Joachim von Ribbentrop*, former champagne salesman, and foreign minister of the Third Reich. A shrewd, selfish, devious-minded diplomat, Ribbentrop worked closely with Hitler in plotting his war of aggression. He served Hitler willingly to the end.

—*Artur von Seyss-Inquart*, betrayer of Austria, and

later *Gauleiter,* or district leader, of the Netherlands. He was ruthless in applying terrorism to the Dutch.

—*Baldur von Schirach,* chief of the Hitler Youth, a young-man-in-a-hurry and ambitious scoundrel, he tried to mold the youth of Germany in Hitler's image. He drove all competing youth groups out of existence.

—*Ernst Kaltenbrunner,* hatchet-faced *Gestapo* chieftain under Heinrich Himmler. He visited the murder camps and saw prisoners killed by hanging, shooting, and gassing, as part of a demonstration.

—*Martin Bormann,* Hitler's deputy party leader, a cruel and vicious taskmaster. During the war he was responsible for the lynching of Allied airmen.

—*Rudolf Franz Hoess,* sullen, pudgy-faced commandant of Auschwitz concentration camp, who streamlined mass murder.

—*Adolf Eichmann,* S.S. officer, who turned Nazi in his teens after a band of Nazi thugs mistook him for a Jew and beat him up. Eichmann helped stage the first deportations of the Jews from Germany in 1933. In 1941, as an S.S. major and chief of the Jewish Central Emigration Office, Eichmann worked on the mass-murder program that took 6,000,000 Jewish lives. He escaped after the war, only to be captured in 1960 in Argentina.

These Nazis, as well as thousands of others not as well-known, committed deeds worse than any credited to the Huns, Goths, and Vandals.

Life in Hitler's Germany

MILLIONS of decent Germans were appalled and disgusted by the Nazi regime. But there was little they could do once Hitler had gained power. The *Gestapo* made Germany one vast prison camp. Any critic of Hitler was fair game for these human bloodhounds. *Gestapo* agents raided homes in the middle of the night to carry off suspects. Some captives vanished forever; others were taken to the dungeons, where they were tortured and beaten to get them to confess to things they had not done.

People grew afraid to talk lest they be denounced to the *Gestapo*. Foreigners who came to Germany began to speak of "the German look," a quick glance back over the shoulder to see if anyone was listening.

The Germans have always had a high respect for law and order. But Hitler made Germany a kind of jungle. Because the top Nazis showed little regard for justice and order, people gave way to buried hates and envy. Those who wanted to get even with others for some real or fancied grievance denounced them to the *Gestapo*. One way to get a man's job, or his apartment, was to betray him to Hitler's secret police. Crimes all the way from holdups to murder were called "politics" in the name of the "national revolution."

Everywhere there was a mad scramble onto the Nazi band wagon. Those who had low numbers in the Nazi Party, showing early membership, took advantage of their good luck. They pounced on the jobs now open because the civil service was purged of all enemies of Hitler, and the professions closed to Jews. Famous professors were thrown out of the universities and their posts taken by Nazis. All the new government officials and mayors were Nazis. Ambitious, jealous men, who until this time had had little or no success in life, suddenly burst forth as the new Nazi rich.

It was an amazing spectacle. Germany, home of thinkers and poets, one of the most civilized of countries, had plunged back to primitive times.

Hitler, the *Fuehrer,* emerged as a kind of blown-up tribal chieftain. His Nazi swastika was a totem, a primitive symbol. He called for the sacrifice of a scapegoat—the Jews—to cleanse the tribe of its miseries. His culture was that of the taboo—forbidden—don't touch—and the voodoo, or black magic.

Hitlerism turned the accepted values of civilized society upside down—indecency became decency, injustice became justice, might became right.

Perhaps the best example of the taboo in Hitler's Germany was the notorious burning of the books. Shortly after Hitler came to power, students and other young people, urged on by Dr. Goebbels, invaded public libraries, dragged out books by "Jewish, Marxist, or Bolshevist" authors, and publicly burned them. In Berlin, the works of some of Germany's greatest writers, such as Heinrich Heine, Sigmund Freud, Emil Ludwig, and others were thrown into a huge bonfire in front of the State Opera House.

Dr. Goebbels was present at the burning. He made a short speech as the books burned: "Never, as today, have young men had the right to cry out. Studies are thriving, spirits awakening. Oh, century, it is a joy to live!"

This circus provoked a wave of disgust around the world. It was something more than an act of juvenile delinquents showing their contempt for books and learning. It was an official act of the Nazi state, promoted by one of its most important leaders.

And what about Nazi voodoo? What about Hitler's black magic?

All the world could see it at the huge Nuremberg rallies. Nuremberg was an old, medieval German city with narrow, crooked streets and gabled houses. It had a glorious history as the citadel of German culture in the sixteenth century. Here Hans Sachs, the cobbler poet, and Albrecht Dürer, the artist, were born.

Each September, Hitler held a great mass meeting of the Nazi Party in Nuremberg. Tens of thousands of Nazis from all over Germany came to pay brassy honor to their high priest. This was the formal gathering of the clans.

Nothing was left to chance. Every trick known to the theater was used to stir up emotions, to drum up warlike passions. "I know what Gibbon meant," said an English visitor, "when he wrote of the clamor of the barbarians."

It was like a savage ballet. Thousands of Nazis marched in perfect order, their heels clicking in unison on the cobblestones. Then came the bands, blaring Nazi .tunes, oom-te-oomting martial music, the men singing as they marched.

Flags and standards merged in a riot of color. The marchers all headed in one direction—toward the huge new stadium where the master would speak to them.

And then came the massing of a forest of Nazis in the vast stadium. At dusk, smoking torches were lit. Searchlights stabbed over the crowd. There was a sense of power, of force, of unity, in the air. There was no *thinking* here. These people were feeling the might and majesty of Adolf Hitler and the Nazi state.

Then, as the excitement mounted to near hysteria, the *Fuehrer* made his entry. Smiling, walking slowly down the open aisle with his cronies, he turned now to the right, now to the left. Up went his arm in the Nazi salute. He mounted the platform.

No one in that great crowd was more moved by the spirit of the moment than Hitler himself. Voice harsh and rasping, he launched into a fighting speech. The Big Chief was telling his people what they must think and do.

This big chief was sure of his destiny. He was the man who had made the famous remark: "I go the way that Providence dictates with the assurance of a sleepwalker."

Before him at Nuremberg were the stiff arms, the

thunderous boots, and the screaming voices of thousands of loyal Nazis. Here was a great mob thinking as one person.

Hitler himself recognized it: "That is the great thing about our movement . . . that these men have outwardly become almost a unit, that actually these members are uniform not only in ideas, but that even the facial expression is almost the same. Look at these laughing eyes, this fanatical enthusiasm, and you will discover how in these faces the same expression has formed, how a hundred thousand men in a movement become a single type."

CHAPTER TWENTY 卐卐卐卐卐卐卐卐卐卐卐卐

The Glorification of Adolf Hitler

IN THIS state of taboo and voodoo Adolf Hitler was the head god. He made certain that everyone would understand that he, and he alone, was boss.

His ambition went even higher than that. "When one comes to visit me," he said, "he should have the feeling that he is meeting the master of the world."

Germany became one vast camp of Hitler saluters. It was wise for all Germans to know how to give that salute. Come to attention, military style, thrust up the right arm as far as it would go, and shout *"Heil* Hitler!" Among friends the salute was not as pompous, just a little lift of the arm.

"Heil!" is the German term for our word "Hail!" Actually, it means salvation, and has been used in the past to apply to relations between man and God. Now in Nazi Germany it took on another meaning. The new German greeting was used instead of "Hello!" or "Good-by!" It was repeated thousands of times morning and night. Everybody used it—the postman, the butcher, the baker, the janitor, the bus conductor, the candy store owner. Everyone used it—or else!

Even children had to give the Nazi greetings. Every child in Germany was expected to say *"Heil* Hitler!" at least fifty times a day, sometimes one hundred times. This was required by law. Study periods at school were opened and closed with the Nazi greeting. *"Heil* Hitler!" cried the Hitler Youth. *"Heil* Hitler!" piped the League of German

Girls. Evening prayers had to be closed with the inevitable *"Heil* Hitler!" Boys and girls were expected to denounce their own parents for failure to use the greeting or for speaking out against it. In the topsy-turvy world of Nazism some children did denounce their mothers and fathers. It meant jail for their parents.

Hitler's picture was everywhere—in classrooms, offices, railroad stations, on street corners. A German could scarcely go anywhere without seeing the face of the *Fuehrer* staring down at him.

Dr. Goebbels' Propaganda Ministry spoke of Hitler in such fantastic terms as these: "We are witnessing the greatest miracle in history. A genius is building the world!" And again: "We heard His voice while Germany slept. His hand has made us a nation again. His hand has led us back to the Fatherland. Our whole life we give to the *Fuehrer."*

Big and little Nazis joined the chorus: "A man of the people, our Adolf Hitler, arose and took German destiny into his strong, clean hands. We love Adolf Hitler because we believe deeply that God has sent him to us to save Germany."

"He alone is never mistaken," said Goebbels. "He is always right. Amazing how great the *Fuehrer* is in his simplicity and how simple is his greatness. He is above us all. He is always like a star above us."

To project this image to the German people Goebbels printed millions of post cards showing Hitler as a giant Siegfried sailing godlike through the air on his way to slay his dragon enemies. This was Hitler's favorite picture.

Rudolf Hess spoke of his master in biblical terms. "And then unto us was born a child in Braunau." His praise went into hysteria:

> *What he does is necessary;*
> *Whatever he does is necessary;*
> *Whatever he does is successful . . . .*
> *Thus clearly the* Fuehrer *has the divine blessing.*

Other Nazis went even further. The Reich Minister for

Church Affairs said that "Adolf Hitler is the true Holy Ghost." Dr. Robert Ley, chief of the Nazi Labor Front, was sure that "the Lord God has sent us Adolf Hitler." Said a Dr. Engelke, known as a "German Christian": "God has manifested himself not in Jesus Christ but in Adolf Hitler."

Special efforts were made to attract children to Adolf Hitler. Here is a poster used for the Hitler Youth:

> We all believe on this earth in Adolf Hitler, our Leader.

> We believe that National Socialism will be the only creed for our people.

> We believe that there is a God in Heaven who created us, leads, and directs us.

> And we believe that this God sent us Adolf Hitler so that Germany should be a Foundation Stone in all Eternity.

Why all this sickening praise? It is an old story, as old as human society itself. Dictators and tyrants are almost always obsessed with fear—fear that they will lose power, fear that underlings will become too powerful, fear that they will be overthrown, fear that they will be killed. To calm these fears they want to be loved as a father. Hence, they try to build up a picture of themselves as great and good men. Hitler used everything for this purpose—word of mouth, press, radio, movies, and the stage.

CHAPTER TWENTY-ONE 卐 卐 卐 卐 卐 卐 卐 卐 卐 卐

"Race" in the Third Reich

The house that Hitler built rested on a shaky foundation —a false theory of race. Millions of Germans were fooled by it.

Hitler claimed that "purity" of race was the most important thing in the world. A people who expected to remain powerful had to keep their blood pure. All civilizations of the world, he said, decayed and fell apart because of racial mixtures. The first aim and purpose of any state, such as Germany, must be *racial purity*. In other words, Germans must be bred like race horses or dogs to see that their blood lines remained pure and unmixed.

Hitler's second basic idea on race was that the so-called Aryan, or Nordic, race was superior to all others. In *Mein Kampf* he divided human beings into two major groups, those he called the *founders of culture,* and those he called the *destroyers of culture.*

According to Hitler, the Aryans were the most important founders of culture. All that is creative was due to the Aryan race. This Aryan race, said Hitler, was composed of tall, blond, thin, blue-eyed, large-boned Germans who looked like gods.

Many Germans were disgusted with this silliness. The perfect Aryan, German humorists said, was "as blond as Hitler, as slim as Goering, and as manly as Goebbels."

The Aryans, Hitler claimed, conquered other peoples early in history. All that we admire on earth, he continued—such as science, art, technical skill and invention

—is the creative product of the Aryan race. Whenever the Aryans allowed their blood to become impure by intermarrying with inferior races, they lost their capacity for civilization and began to die out.

And who, according to Hitler, were the destroyers of culture?

Why, the Jews, of course. They are non-Aryans. The Jewish "race," said Hitler, is exactly the opposite of the Aryan "race." He made a long series of ridiculous charges against the Jews. He said that they had no culture of their own, but stole their culture from others. He charged that they were parasites, traitors, who wanted to dominate the whole world.

Once in power, Hitler outlined a whole "science" of race for the guidance of German scholars. The men who preached this science were more quacks than scholars. One of them, a Dr. Hermann Gauch, seriously wrote that "birds can learn to talk better than other animals because their mouths are Nordic in structure." "Non-Nordic, or Jewish animals," he said, "can only make confused sounds, like barking, snoring, sniffling, squeaking."

One Nazi newspaper claimed that "only the fruits of the German earth can create German blood." Therefore, Germans must not eat lemons because they are grown on foreign soil. They must eat rhubarb that was grown in Germany!

A local law in Frankfurt-am-Main during the Nazi regime held that "Jewish dogs" must take their daily walks out at six o'clock in the morning, but "Aryan dogs" could sleep until nine o'clock, so that Aryan and Jewish dogs would not mix their blood!

And what was a Jewish dog? It was a dog that belonged to a Jewish family!

Sad to say, this racial nonsense became law in the Nazi Third Reich. It was the code by which Germans were forced to live for twelve years.

This is not the place to argue Adolf Hitler's ideas on race. But it is fair to note at this point the basic truths of what scientists believe about race:

1. We speak of a race as a species or division of mankind. Thus, there are five main races: the white, black, brown, red, and yellow. But that is as far as we can go.

2. There is no such thing as a "pure" race. The peoples of the world are mixed so much that a pure race would be impossible.

3. There is no such thing as a superior race. No one race has ever proved itself superior to any other.

4. There is no such thing as a German race or a British race. It would be just as silly to say that there is an American race! All these peoples, whether Germans or British, or Americans, form a nation, not a race.

5. There is no such thing as a Jewish race. It would be just as foolish to speak of a Catholic or Moslem race! These are religions, not races.

6. There is no such thing as an Aryan race. Aryans are merely people who belong to the same language group. Thus, Germans, British, French, Italians, and Persians are all Aryan-speaking peoples.

Hitler denied all this. In *Mein Kampf* he said that the state "must place race as the central point of the life of the community, and must guard the preservation of its purity."

Again, he said, "The race question is the key not only to world history but also to human culture in general."

Hitler believed that all weak and sickly children should be killed. "If Germany would have a million children a year and do away with seven hundred thousand of the weakest of these, it might even result in an increase of strength."

Hitler's ideas were jungle ideas; his revolt was a revolt against human reason.

CHAPTER TWENTY-TWO 卐 卐 卐 卐 卐 卐 卐 卐 卐 卐

Hatred for the Jews

HITLER'S capacity for hate was almost limitless, but above all else he hated the Jews. It was a deep-rooted hatred that never left him during his entire life. In *Mein Kampf* he wrote: "The black-haired Jewish youth lies for hours in ambush, a Satanic joy in his face, for the unsuspecting girl whom he pollutes with his blood and steals her own race."

Hitler blamed the Jews for all Germany's ills.

Item: The Jews were traitors who stabbed the Germans in the back and made them lose World War I.

Item: The Jews were communists.

Item: The Jews were capitalists.

Item: The Jews wanted to run the entire world.

As proof that the Jews wanted to dominate the world, Hitler reprinted millions of copies of a pamphlet called *The Protocols of the Elders of Zion.* According to this little booklet, Jewish leaders from all over the world come to Switzerland once a year to meet in a cemetery and tell how each one is getting along in his campaign to control the life of his own country.

The *Protocols* was an absurd forgery from beginning to end. Scholars had long since shown it to be a fraud written by bigoted anti-Semites. But, using the technique of the big lie, Hitler duped many unthinking people into accepting the *Protocols* as gospel truth.

Hitler pushed his anti-Semitic campaign during the years when he was striving for political power. Nazi underlings striving for promotion, tried to outdo one another in attacking the Jews.

The worst Jew baiter of all was Julius Streicher, who used his scandal sheet, *Der Stuermer,* to attack the Jews in screaming black and red headlines. He charged that Jewish rabbis drank Christian blood in their rituals. Jewish doctors, he said, could not be trusted because they gave dope to German girls. "The Jew," he shouted, "is the devil in human form."

In the Jews, Hitler found scapegoats for all Germany's troubles. "The wretched Jew," he said, "enemy of the human race, is the cause of all our suffering." He wanted every Jew out of Germany.

On April 7, 1933, a Hitler law removed all "non-Aryans" from public office. "A person," stated the law, "shall be known as a non-Aryan who has non-Aryan, particularly Jewish, grandparents. It is enough if one parent or grandparent is a non-Aryan." At first this did not apply to Jewish public servants who had been at the front in World War I, or who had lost fathers or sons in the war. But later even these were included in the anti-Jewish laws.

More than 100,000 Jews in Germany bore arms in World War I. Some 35,000 Jews received war medals; 23,000 Jewish soldiers were promoted to officer rank. But none of this impressed Hitler.

Within a few years Nazi Germany was purged of Jewish doctors, lawyers, judges, teachers, and nurses. Jewish businessmen were forced to sell out at a loss. Jews were barred from the stage, the movies, journalism. Jewish artists were allowed to appear only before Jewish audiences. Nazi students drove Jewish professors from the classrooms with catcalls and jeers. Jewish stores were picketed. Jewish children were taunted. And through the streets marched the storm troopers singing:

When Jewish blood spurts from under the knife,
Things will be twice as good as before.

In late 1935, Hitler had another series of laws passed against the Jews. The so-called Nuremberg, or Ghetto, Laws took German citizenship away from the Jews on the ground that they were of "non-German blood." A Jew was defined as anyone "who is descended from one or two grandparents who racially, were full Jews." For the first time in history prejudice and bias were put directly into the laws of a great modern state.

Law after law directed against the Jews appeared on the statute books. Any Jew who did not have a name that "sounded Jewish" was forced to add "Israel" or "Sarah" to his or her name. The idea was to make the Jews appear foolish and foreign to Germans.

In the fall of 1938 came further tragedy. The Nazis rounded up thousands of Polish Jews, living in Germany, herded them into railroad cars, sent them to the Polish border, and then forced them, frightened and freezing, to walk across into Polish territory. The Polish government promptly said it would do the same thing to Germans living in Poland. This was language Hitler understood. He stopped—for the time being.

One of the Jews deported by Hitler sent a post card describing his ordeal to his seventeen-year-old son living in Paris. The boy, Herschel Greenspan, brooded over the injustice done his father until he reached the decision to go to the German embassy and kill the German ambassador. Instead, he shot the third secretary, who died a few days later.

Hitler was furious when he heard this. In a matter of hours, Jews all over Germany were viciously attacked. Mobs roamed the streets, burning Jewish synagogues, desecrating Jewish cemeteries, attacking and beating helpless Jews in their homes. Brutal storm troopers forced elderly Jews to clean the streets on their hands and knees. Windows of Jewish storekeepers were smashed.

All the German Jews were held responsible for the act of a hysterical Jewish boy in Paris. Hitler fined the Jews $400,000,000 by taking twenty per cent of their property away from them. Jewish shopkeepers were made to repair, at their own expense, all the damage done to their stores during the Nazi riots.

Thereafter, German Jews were not allowed to walk on certain streets. They were not allowed to sit on park benches. They were forbidden to drive automobiles. Public markets, playgrounds, and winter resorts were strictly off-bounds to them. So that none might try to pass for what they were not, all Jews were commanded to wear yellow Stars of David to identify themselves.

The whole world was appalled by the news from inside Germany. Jews in other countries began to boycott German goods. The result was that German Jews were treated still more harshly.

Refusing to endure the insults and curses, thousands of Jews fled Germany to seek freedom and a decent life elsewhere. Many famous Jews, including the great scientist Albert Einstein, left German soil forever. But the majority, penniless, unable to obtain visas for other countries, sank into despair in the ghettos set apart for them. They could venture out from these ghettos only at their own peril.

During World War II, Hitler's hatred of the Jews reached the point of mental illness. He ordered that "the Jewish question be solved for all time." Any Jew in Europe the Nazis could capture was to be put to death.

As many as six million Jews fell victim to Hitler's insanity. Many died in the Warsaw ghetto, others in Hitler's concentration camps. Moving pictures show S.S. troops looking on with pleasure as Jews with swollen knees and fleshless legs dropped to the ground and died. Other films reveal lines of corpse-filled carts being pushed to the edge of lime pits, where bodies were sent sprawling down a chute. Millions of Jews died in gas ovens.

The whole sickening story came out after the war. It was worse than Dante's Inferno, probably the blackest page in the history of mankind.

The Anti-Christ

HITLER'S racial mania and his anti-Semitism laid the groundwork for his assault on Christianity. He rejected Christianity as an alien idea, foreign to the pure racial culture of the Germans. "Antiquity," said Hitler, "was better than modern times because it did not know Christianity and syphilis."

Here was Hitler's criticism of Christianity:

1. It was a religion that sided with everything weak and low.

2. It was purely Jewish and Oriental in origin. Christians "bend their backs to the sound of church bells and crawl to the cross of a foreign God."

3. The religion began 2,000 years ago among sick, exhausted, and despairing men who had lost their belief in life.

4. Christian ideas of "forgiveness of sin," "resurrection," and "salvation" were just nonsense.

5. The Christian idea of mercy was dangerous. One must never extend mercy to his enemies. "Mercy is an un-German conception."

6. Christian "love" was silly; love paralyzes.

7. The Christian idea of equality of all human beings meant that the inferior, the ill, the crippled, the criminal, and the weak were protected.

Therefore, Hitler said, Christianity, just as much as Judaism, was opposed to the Nazi ideals he had set for Germany. He did not want to destroy Christianity altogether.

What he tried to do was to corrupt it and twist its meaning.

It was not long before Hitler became involved in a war with the Protestant and Catholic churches. There were twenty-nine different Protestant churches in Germany, all of which Hitler tried to bring under his control. At first he did nothing, biding his time until he was ready to strike. Then, in 1935, he decreed the supremacy of the Nazi state over the Protestant church. He closed down church schools and took over church property. He drove many pastors from their pulpits and forbade others to preach. Those who dared to speak their minds were sent to out-of-the-way villages. He would destroy the strength of Protestantism by a slow process of erosion.

Some Protestant pastors, Lutheran and Calvinist, went along with Hitler and the Nazis. But many others refused to bow to the swastika. The celebrated Heidelberg professor and leader of the German Protestants, Dr. Karl Barth, refused to take an oath to Hitler. He was removed from his post in 1935. "I was a professor of theology for ten years at Bonn University on the Rhine," he wrote later from Switzerland, "until I refused to open my lectures on God each day by raising my arm and saying, '*Heil* Hitler!' I could not do that. It would have been blasphemy. And so I was compelled to come to Basle University."

Most outspoken of the Protestant pastors was Dr. Martin Niemoeller, minister in the wealthy Berlin suburb of Dahlem. His was an unusual career—he had been a submarine officer in World War I. In 1937, he was arrested and tried secretly on a charge of sedition. The court freed him of all major charges, but he was arrested again by the *Gestapo* and sent off to a concentration camp. But Hitler never succeeded in taming Niemoeller.

Hitler's persecution of Protestant pastors backfired on the Nazis. The religion actually became stronger. People jammed the churches that once were empty. It was the only way many Germans could show their disgust with the Nazi regime.

When he came to power in 1933, Hitler at first decided to remain on good terms with the Catholic Church. He had, after all, been born a Catholic. He concluded a

Reich Concordat, or treaty, with the church, guaranteeing the integrity of the Catholic faith and safeguarding the church's rights. Catholic schools, youth groups, and cultural societies were not to be disturbed if they kept out of politics.

The Catholic bishops tried hard to remain on good terms with Hitler and the Nazis. But underneath there was a strong hostility that grew still stronger as one by one Hitler broke the terms of the Concordat.

Soon the drum fire of Nazi propaganda began to be directed toward the Catholics. Leading Nazis began to speak of the enemies of Germany as "Judea and Rome," that is, Jews and Catholics. The Catholic Church, they charged, was an international organization, loyal to the Pope instead of to Hitler. To the Nazis, Christian ethics were more suitable for a slave society than a strong Aryan nation like Germany.

Why was Hitler opposed to the Catholics? One reason was that the Catholic Church was truly international. The name itself means universal. Such a church could not accept the superiority of any people.

Another reason for Hitler's opposition to the Catholics was that he claimed the right to control the whole education of German children, denying the right of the Catholic clergy to guide the spirit and soul of its youth. Most of all, Hitler was opposed to the basic teachings of Christ—especially the golden rule of doing to others as we would have them do to us, and he could not endure the concept of peace on earth.

The ensuing struggle between Hitler and the Catholic Church was marked by violence. Hitler arrested monks and nuns and accused them of smuggling gold out of Germany. He censored the Catholic press. He forbade Catholic religious processions, and banned pastoral letters. He tried to force Catholic boys into the Hitler Youth.

The Catholics fought back. Michael Cardinal von Faulhaber, the Archbishop of Munich, refused to give in and courageously defied the Nazis. To forestall his arrest, the Church made him a papal legate in 1934, which gave him diplomatic immunity from arrest.

On March 21, 1937, Pope Pius XI issued an encyclical, or papal letter, on Germany titled *Mit brennender Sorge,*

"With Burning Anxiety." The letter, which was read from every Catholic pulpit in Germany, accused Hitler of breaking his agreement with the Church, and stated that he had exposed Catholics to "violence as illegal as it is inhuman." "With paternal emotion," said the Pope, "we feel and suffer profoundly with those who have paid such a great price for their attachment to Christ and the Church."

Hitler's reply was a new series of trials of monks and lay brothers on charges of immorality and currency violations.

Instead of the "weak Christian religion," Hitler wanted a German "National Church" with an Aryan clergy and Aryan ethics. This was what he called "Positive Christianity," what was to be the new German Christian religion.

Here was the program of Hitler's new "German Christianity":

1. Throw out the Old Testament—it is a Jewish book. Also throw out parts of the New Testament.

2. Christ must be regarded not as Jewish, but as a Nordic martyr put to death by the Jews, a kind of warrior who by His death saved the world from Jewish domination.

3. Adolf Hitler is the new Messiah sent to earth to rescue the world from the Jews.

4. The swastika succeeds the cross as the symbol of German Christianity.

5. German land, German blood, German soul, German art—these four must become the most sacred things of all to the German Christian.

Speaking for the German National Church, Professor Ernst Bergmann said: "Either we have a German God or none at all. The international God flies with the strongest bombing squadrons—and they are not on the German side. We cannot kneel before a God who pays more attention to the French than to us. We Germans have been forsaken by the Christian God. He is not a just, supernatural God, but a political party God of the others. It is because we believed in Him and not in our German God that we were defeated in the struggle of the nations."

Christians all over the world were repelled by this

Nazi "Positive Christianity," precisely the opposite of what they believed.

Some Nazi leaders, anxious to be in Hitler's good graces, repudiated Christianity completely. Instead, they wanted to set up a pagan cult of "blood, race, and soil." They would go back to the dark ritual and dramatic rites of their ancestors.

The New Pagans resurrected Odin, Thor, and the old gods of primitive Teutons before Christ's time. Instead of the Old Testament they adopted Nordic sagas and fairy tales. They set up a new trinity for worship— *bravery, loyalty,* and *physical force.*

"We believe," said a Nazi pagan, "that the Lord God has sent us Adolf Hitler so that Germany shall be established for all eternity." In some churches Hitler's photograph was placed on the altars, and flames were lit before the picture. This was supposed to arouse "the good old healthy Nordic instincts."

There was even a hymn for the new German Faith Movement:

> *The time of the Cross has gone now,*
> *The Sun-wheel shall arise,*
> *And so, with God, we shall be free at last*
> *And give our people their honor back.*

Hitler did not openly come to the support of the new paganism. He was too shrewd a politician to do that. But he was not opposed to its ideas. In 1937, he awarded the National Prize, Germany's version of the Nobel Prize, to Alfred Rosenberg, foe of Christianity and leader of the Neo-Pagans. Rosenberg, Nazi philosopher, wanted a return to the old Teutonic religion of fire and sword.

CHAPTER TWENTY-FOUR

God-Men for the Future 卐卐卐卐卐卐卐卐卐卐卐

"Whoever has the youth has the future."
ADOLF HITLER

HITLER had some very definite ideas about education. "I begin with the young," he said. "We older ones are used up. We are rotten to the marrow.

"But my magnificent youngsters! Are there any finer ones in the world? Look at these young men and boys! What material! With them I can make a new world.

"My teaching will be hard. Weakness will be knocked out of them. A violently active, dominating, brutal youth —that is what I am after. Youth must be indifferent to pain. There must be no weakness or tenderness in it. I want to see once more in its eyes the gleam of pride and independence of the beast of prey.

"I will have no intellectual training. Knowledge is ruin to my young men. I would have them learn only what takes their fancy. But one thing they must learn—self-command! They shall learn to overcome their fear of death under the severest tests.

"This is the heroic stage of youth. Out of it will come the creative man, the god-man!"

Until Hitler came to power, German schools had the respect of the entire world. The teaching was dignified, the work was thorough and exact. Schools all over the world were modeled after those of Germany.

By the time Hitler was through with his "reforms," he

had destroyed the reputation of German schools. They were now among the worst in the world.

Hitler forced two basic ideas on the entire school system. First, there must be burnt into the heart and brain of youth the sense of race. Second, German youth must be made ready for war, educated for victory or death.

The first book the German child saw when he was out of kindergarten was the *Primer*. On the cover was a typical Nazi caricature of the Jew, with the words: *Trust no fox on the green heath! And no Jew on his oath!*

On the inside pages the children were given pictures of marching and camp life:

> *He who wants to be a soldier,*
> *That one must have a weapon,*
> *Which he must load with powder,*
> *And with a good hard bullet.*
> *Little fellow, if you want to be a recruit,*
> *Take good care of this little song!*

It was much the same in the higher grades. Here the approved textbook on race was Hermann Gauch's *New Elements of Racial Research,* with passages such as this: "The animal world can be reclassified into Nordic men and lower animals (Jews). We are thus able to establish the following principle: there exist no physical or psychological characteristics that would justify a differentiation of mankind from the animal world. The only differences that exist are those between Nordic man, on the one hand, and animals, in general, including non-Nordic men, or sub-men (who are a transitional species), on the other hand."

In other words—Germans are human beings, Jews are animals!

Mathematics for German students was supposed to express the Nordic fighting spirit. Here is a problem from a high school arithmetic book: *An airplane flies at the rate of 240 kilometers per hour to a place at a distance of 210 kilometers in order to drop bombs. When may it be expected to return if the dropping of bombs takes 7.5 minutes?*

So it went through the entire curriculum. Study of

the German language meant German nationalism. Study of religion meant lessons in National Socialism. Study in physics and chemistry meant Nazi physics and Nazi chemistry.

Even the universities were invaded by the spirit of Nazism. Distinguished professors were hounded from their jobs, and their places taken by young, inexperienced Nazis. The great German universities, known to all the world as the finest institutions of higher learning, plunged to the low level of Nazi art and science.

Hitler was not satisfied, however, in controlling only the school system. He wanted to supervise the entire life of his German boys and girls. He set up two organizations for boys: the *Jungvolk*, or Young Boys, from eight to fourteen years of age, and the *Hitler Jugend*, or Hitler Youth, from ages fourteen to eighteen. At first only those who wanted to be members were taken into these clubs. But by 1936 a law required all German boys to enter the Hitler Youth.

The Hitler Youth were taught defense sports, physical education, and rifle practice.

Defense sports included formation drill, reading of maps, estimating distances, laying false trails, camouflaging, scouting, sketching, pitching tents, and direction finding at night.

Physical education included tumbling, boxing, swimming, cross-country and endurance running, Indian club throwing, and marching with full equipment.

Rifle practice included study of firearms, care of weapons, shooting, positions for firing, activity as recorders, and munition-passers.

The main purpose of the Hitler Youth Clubs was to train the body so that the boys would become hard as steel, but above all to teach military order, discipline, and knowledge.

The Hitler Youth were expected to sing as they marched to martial music in a sea of flags. Here is the chorus of the "Song of the Hitler Youth":

Our flag flutters before us, as into the future
We move man for man.
We are marching for Hitler through night

And through danger,
With the flag of youth for freedom and bread.

How much marching were these boys required to do? A thirteen-year-old had to march eleven miles a day! A sixteen-year-old had to march fifteen and a half miles a day, carrying an eleven-pound load. Thousands of boys broke down because of these long marches on hard roads. Others suffered from flat feet for the rest of their lives.

Many parents protested. Often the boys were up until midnight carrying flaming torches at Hitler meetings. But it was dangerous to speak out too loudly in the Third Reich.

The Hitler Youth were not supposed to think for themselves. They were to take orders blindly, obediently, and without question. And to be sure they knew the right answers they had to repeat over and over again such mottoes as:

THE *Fuehrer* IS ALWAYS RIGHT! OUR LIFE FOR
THE *Fuehrer*!
WE SWEAR THAT OUR LIVES BELONG TO THE REICH AND
OUR BLOOD TO THE *Fuehrer*!
FREEDOM AND LIFE ARE ONLY FOR THOSE WHO
ARE READY TO FIGHT!

To provide for the education of future Nazi leaders, Hitler set up thirty-two special schools. These were for the chosen ones, the Nazi elite, the leaders of the future. Cadets were sent to these schools at the age of twelve to become "supermen." They studied in romantic medieval castles. Both students and teachers wore Hitler Youth uniforms. The curriculum stressed racialism, physical exercise, obedience, loyalty to Hitler.

From the ages of ten to fourteen the German girl was a member of the *Jungmaedels,* or Young Girls. From fourteen to twenty-one she was in the *Bund Deutscher Maedchen,* or League of German Girls. In both these clubs she learned two basic lessons: to prepare herself to be a mother, and to get ready for war.

"Maidens, practice sport!" Hitler commanded. He wanted German girls to grow up strong and healthy for one reason—to bring new German warriors into the world.

He wanted no training for the minds of his Nazi maidens. "The one absolute aim of female education," he wrote in *Mein Kampf*, "must be with a view to the future mother."

German girls were required to spend many hours swimming, diving, folk dancing, and practicing gymnastics. Again and again they heard the words, "The most important thing in the world is to become a mother. The *Fuehrer* demands this and nothing else from all German girls. You must perform this important service for the Fatherland."

Whether a girl was married or not made no difference. Whether she was in love with the boy was not important. The only thing that mattered was that both parents-to-be should be "racially pure" and in good health. The childless woman, whether or not unmarried, had no place in the Third Reich.

The result was a great rise in the number of children born out of wedlock. Thousands of unmarried German girls, some as young as fourteen, became mothers. Heartbroken parents, unable to protest, looked on in horror. What could they say? What could they do?

The second aim for the German girl was to be prepared for war. She had to learn first aid, air raid protection, and such housekeeping tasks as how to prepare a one-pot dish. She had to be ready to serve as a nurse for soldiers in the field, or as "a defender of the homeland."

German girls became second-class citizens. Their hope of higher education was cut off. (Within three years after Hitler came to power the number of girls in German universities dropped from twenty thousand to ten thousand, a decline of fifty per cent.) Their hopes of becoming doctors and lawyers were ruined. Their only function was to breed soldiers for Hitler.

In a way it was most ironic. Hitler shouted that the German people needed more *Lebensraum,* living space. There were too many people in Germany; she must expand to take care of her excess people. But at the same time Hitler called for more and more children.

It was an *excuse for aggression.* Hitler was preparing his young people for war.

The Road to War, 1934–1939

As SOON AS he became dictator, Hitler turned his attention to the problem of acquiring great power in Europe and the world.

What did he want?

He wanted Germany to rearm and become as strong or even stronger than all other European powers.

He wanted all Germany's colonies given back to her.

He wanted those lands Germany had lost in 1918–1919 returned—lands such as Alsace-Lorraine and the Saar region. He wanted Danzig as well as the Polish Corridor, which had been given to Poland by the Treaty of Versailles.

He wanted land in the east, in the rich plains of Poland, in the Ukraine areas of the Soviet Union.

But that was not all. Hitler wanted a Greater Germany to include all the Germans who lived outside the Third Reich—especially Germans of his homeland Austria, and the Sudeten Germans in Czechoslovakia. In the 1860's, the great Prussian Chancellor Otto von Bismarck had excluded Austria from the German state he was building. Hitler would right that "historical wrong."

He had it all worked out. After building the Nazi New Order in Europe, he would conquer the "inferior races" in the East and make them slave workers for the German *Herrenvolk,* the ruling people. The slaves would be given just enough food to keep them alive. Polish intellectuals would be wiped out; the Jews would be exterminated.

And while this was going on, the Nazis would extend their Brown Network in South America and the rest of the world. A proud day would come when the Nazi Third Reich would take "the place of the old decaying British Empire."

Most of this Hitler explained in his book, *Mein Kampf*. The blueprint was there. But the statesmen of the world paid little attention. They did not believe that Hitler really intended to carry out these fantastic ideas once he came to power in Germany.

From the beginning Hitler was incredibly lucky. His opponents, the statesmen of Britain and France, wanted only one thing—to stay out of war. But Hitler was willing to risk war. He was bold—and he got his war.

The first step was to rearm and make Germany strong. The Treaty of Versailles had limited Germany's army to 100,000 men, a small navy, and no air force. Claiming that Germany had been mistreated, Hitler withdrew from the Disarmament Conference, which was meeting to reduce armaments for all nations. At the same time he announced that Germany was leaving the League of Nations.

Then, while busily making speeches about peace, Hitler saw to it that the factories of Germany worked day and night to build up a strong war machine.

As early as 1934, a year after he came to power, Hitler tried his first gamble. He would take Austria by *Anschluss*, or union, even though this had been forbidden at Versailles. On July 25, 1934, Austrian Nazis shot Chancellor Engelbert Dollfuss of Austria and let him bleed to death by denying him a doctor's attention. Now, Hitler was ready to march into Austria. But the Italian Fascist dictator, Mussolini, furious because Hitler had broken his promise not to invade Austria, sent Italian troops to the frontier of Austria to guard that country's independence.

Hitler backed down. He was shrewd enough to know that this time he had overreached himself. He would bide his time while making Germany strong.

In March, 1935, Hitler announced that Germany would build a peacetime army of thirty-six divisions, or 550,000 men. This was in direct violation of the Treaty of Versailles. The Great Powers protested mildly. Hitler answered them with honeyed words about peace, appeals to "reason," and demands for "justice." He went on to build his army.

A year later, in March, 1936, Hitler ordered German troops to march into the Rhineland. This, too, was a violation of the Versailles peace treaty. The *Fuehrer's* advisers warned him to be careful. Surely, they said, France, with Europe's finest army, would march against the Germans.

But Hitler was certain of his star of destiny. The Germans marched, and the French did nothing.

Later Hitler said: "The forty-eight hours after the march into the Rhineland were the most nerve-wracking of my life. If the French had moved, we would have had to withdraw with our tail between our legs—for we were militarily weak."

When on July 18, 1936, civil war broke out in Spain, Hitler gave aid to Franco and the Spanish Fascists. During the bloody civil war, he sent his *Luftwaffe,* or air force pilots, and tankmen to help Franco and to get experience under battle conditions. It was a dress rehearsal for World War II.

Mussolini, too, helped Franco. This common policy was one of the main props for the Rome-Berlin Axis agreement, beginning October 27, 1936. Italy and Germany joined in a common front against Bolshevism and the Western powers. Here was a solid bloc of 115 million people devoted to the task of obtaining living space for two "have-not" nations.

By this time it was becoming clear to all the world that Hitler wanted war. This was the man who said: "For the good of the German people we must wish for a war every fifteen or twenty years."

But at the same time he was saying: "I am not crazy enough to want a war."

With one as erratic as this and as intoxicated with power, no reasonable peace was possible, no promise secure, no agreement long-lasting. Hitler was obsessed with the idea that the superior German "race" was going to rule the world. He was getting ready to smash his way to power in Europe and the rest of the world.

A fine German citizen recognized it and spoke out. He was Thomas Mann, the greatest German novelist of his day. Unable to live under the Nazis, he left his homeland and remained abroad, which infuriated the Nazis.

In December, 1936, the dean of Bonn University sent a letter to "Herr Thomas Mann, Writer," informing him that his name had been struck from the roll of honorary doctors. Mann replied in a letter that has since become famous. It told the whole world that Adolf Hitler was preparing for war:

> I have spent four years as an exile. Had I remained in Germany I should probably not be alive today. From time to time I must give free vent to my abysmal disgust at what is happening at home—the contemptible words and still more contemptible deeds.
>
> To what a pass, in less than four years, have they brought Germany! Ruined, sucked dry body and soul by armaments with which they threaten the whole world, loved by nobody, regarded with fear and aversion by all.
>
> The meaning and purpose of the National Socialist State is this alone and can be only this: to make the German people ready for the 'coming war' by ruthless oppression; to make of them an instrument of war, without a single critical thought, driven by a blind and fanatical ignorance.
>
> No, this war is impossible. Germany cannot wage it. . . .
>
> Why these robbers and murderers? Why isolation, world hostility, lawlessness, intellectual interdict, cultural darkness, and every other evil? Why not Germany's return to the European system, with freedom, justice, well-being, and human decency?
>
> I close this letter with a brief and fervent prayer: God help our darkened and desecrated country and teach it to make its peace with the world and with itself!
>
> THOMAS MANN

Thomas Mann spoke for all those Germans who were disgusted by what Adolf Hitler had done to Germany and what he intended to do in the future.

But Hitler paid no attention. He went ahead with his program of making a strong Germany. Everything was sacrificed to this one end—to make Germany ready for war.

The record proves that Hitler wanted the war. On November 5, 1937, almost two years before the invasion of Poland, he had a meeting with his military leaders. His adjutant, Colonel Friedrich Hossbach, wrote down the minutes of the meeting. The Hossbach Document, which was later used at the Nuremberg trials, tells a damning story.

At this meeting the *Fuehrer* told his generals that Germany needed space for her people. Therefore, he said, the question for Germany was where the "greatest possible conquest can be made at lowest cost."

Hitler then said that, if he were still alive, it would be his decision to solve the German space problem "no later than 1943–1945." Then he gave the exact way to do it: "To better our military position, it must be our first aim to conquer Czechoslovakia and Austria together, in order to remove any threat from our flanks in case we move westward. Once Czechoslovakia is conquered, we can more easily rely on the Poles staying neutral while we fight the French. Our agreement with Poland will be good only as long as we remain strong."

Hitler was not gossiping at a *Kaffeeklatsch*. Present at this meeting were Hermann Goering, commander-in-chief of the *Luftwaffe;* Konstantin von Neurath, the German foreign minister; Field Marshal Werner von Blomberg, the German war minister; Colonel-General Werner von Fritsch, commander-in-chief of the German Army; and Admiral Erich Raeder, commander-in-chief of the German Navy. These were Hitler's top commanders.

He talked to them for hours. Germany's problem, Hitler said, could be solved only by force. The question was "when" and "how?"

Two members of the German High Command present at the Hossbach meeting opposed Hitler's risking war with Great Britain and France. They said nothing at the time, but Hitler knew he had to get rid of them.

Field Marshal von Blomberg, minister of war, had fallen in love with and married a young woman of bad reputation. This gave Hitler the chance to remove the officer who had not shown enough enthusiasm for the *Fuehrer* and his plans.

Next, on a false morals charge, Hitler relieved Army Commander-in-chief von Fritsch of his command. When war broke out von Fritsch deliberately allowed himself to be killed at the front.

Hitler retired other senior generals and purged high German statesmen and diplomats until all those who opposed him were out of the way. There were plenty of yes-men ready to do the *Fuehrer's* work.

With his position stronger at home, Hitler sent for the Austrian Chancellor, Kurt von Schuschnigg, and threatened to blast his country into bits unless von Schuschnigg agreed to a union with Germany.

"Do you want to make another Spain of Austria?" Hitler demanded. "Austria is alone. Neither France nor England will lift a finger to save you!"

This time Mussolini gave his blessing. "Please tell Mussolini," a delighted Hitler told his ambassador in Rome, "that I shall never forget him for this. I thank him ever so much. Never, never shall I forget!"

At daybreak on March 12, 1938, German troops marched across the border into Austria. Within hours Hitler was being driven through the streets of Linz while thousands cheered. Adolf Hitler was home at last—a hero. On the following day he made a triumphant entry into Vienna.

A plebiscite, or vote, was held in both Germany and Austria under Nazi direction. Exactly 90.08 per cent of Germans voted approval; in Austria it was 99.75 per cent. It was not healthy to vote against *Anschluss*.

"This is the proudest hour of my life," said Hitler.

The annexation of Austria was a great victory for the Nazi leader. At no cost to Germany, Hitler had seized the key to the Danube River, isolated Czechoslovakia, and also dealt a blow to French influence in the Balkans. Most important of all, he had shown the world once again that he could defy the Western powers without fearing any reprisals.

In England, Winston Churchill, who at this time did not have political power, warned that German aggression in Europe had begun.

It was easy to guess where Hitler would turn next. He had hated the Czechs since his days in Vienna. And he hated the new democratic state of Czechoslovakia, ally of France and Russia. He had already said that he would annex that state as the next step in his program. And the ease with which he had taken Austria encouraged him to go ahead.

He planned everything very carefully. Inside Czechoslovakia were over three million Sudeten Germans, a strong and loud minority. Also there was a Czech Nazi Party under the leadership of Konrad Henlein. Hitler started the drums rolling in his usual fashion, shouting to the world that the poor Germans inside Czechoslovakia were being cruelly and viciously treated.

Soon there were Nazi-inspired riots inside Czechoslovakia. Hitler promised the Sudeten Germans that he would not nelgect them. Germans everywhere could depend on him, he said. He would strike down the Czechs who were mistreating his German comrades.

This saber-rattling frightened the British Prime Minister, Neville Chamberlain. He decided to go to Germany to plead with Hitler for peace. Three times the sixty-nine-year-old Briton flew to Germany on his mission of peace.

"Three hundred Sudeten Germans have been killed," Hitler told Chamberlain. "I do not care whether there is a world war or not. I am determined to settle it and to settle it soon." He said he would march into the Sudetenland on October 1, 1938.

War seemed certain now. But Britain and France were not ready for war. On September 30, 1938, Prime Minister Chamberlain, Premier Édouard Daladier of France, Mussolini, and Hitler met and signed the Munich Pact. The little democratic state of Czechoslovakia was sold down the river. Hitler had his Sudetenland, and soon he would have all of Czechoslovakia.

This was the high point of appeasement, the act of sacrificing principles to avoid aggression. Chamberlain flew home showing a signed paper and stating that he had brought "peace for our time."

True, peace had been preserved, but the Czechs had paid the bill. Winston Churchill called it "a disaster of first magnitude."

Hitler was annoyed at being denied a brief military campaign against the Czechs, but otherwise he was happy. He had made Germany strong. In five years he had raised her from a lowly nation to a great world power.

"I shall go down in history as the greatest German of all time," he boasted.

Hitler had also won a great victory at home. It was all astonishing. The *Fuehrer* had dealt one crippling blow after another to the system of Versailles. The West— Britain and France—seemed paralyzed. Many Germans, who at first had been a bit skeptical about this comic-opera dictator, began to see in him a great leader, one who would guide them to a glorious future.

The Nazis were joyful. "You see," they said, "we told you the glorious *Fuehrer* can do no wrong!"

What the Nazis did not see was that it was impossible to do what Hitler was doing without war. They did not know what was happening to them.

On March 14, 1939, the German Army marched into Prague, capital of Czechoslovakia. The whole country was now under Hitler's heel.

At this point the British gave up trying to appease Hitler. His promises could not be trusted. The man was a liar. Britain and France made it clear to all the world that if Hitler moved again—against either Danzig or Poland— there would be war. This was not couched in vague language difficult to understand or interpret. It was plain, clear, simple.

Throughout the summer of 1939, Hitler remained quiet, hoping that London and Paris would let down their guard. His eye was on Poland. He guessed that he would have to fight Britain and France if he invaded his neighbor to the east, but he was prepared to take the risk. It would be a struggle to the death.

"It is no longer a question of right or wrong," he said, "but life or death for eighty million human beings." And by human beings he meant the Germans.

Again Hitler revealed that he wanted war. He told his commanding officers at another secret conference: "I am only afraid that at the last minute some Schweinhund (filthy fellow) will produce a plan of mediation."

On August 23, 1939, Nazi Germany and Soviet Russia, mortal enemies, signed a pact of friendship. It was a diplomatic bombshell. The two countries agreed to divide Poland between them. This was Stalin's reply to the West, whom he suspected of trying to turn the Nazi barbarians against Bolshevik Russia.

During the afternoon of September 1, 1939, Nevile Henderson, the British ambassador in Berlin, brought to Hitler a demand from Prime Minister Chamberlain that Germany suspend all aggressive action and withdraw from Poland. Otherwise "His Majesty's Government in the United Kingdom will without hesitation fulfill their obligations to Poland."

Hitler was angered by this letter. He made no reply, but privately he said, "I am fifty years old, and prefer war now to when I shall be fifty-three or sixty."

German troops were already moving into Poland. Hitler spoke to the *Reichstag:* "Last night for the first time regular soldiers of the Polish Army fired shots on our territory. Since 5:45 A.M., we have been returning their fire."

Again the big lie! There had been a faked attack on the German Gleiwitz radio station by S.S. members dressed in Polish uniforms.

He was dramatic. "Once again," he proclaimed, "I have put on the tunic that was to me the holiest and most beloved of garments. I shall take it off only after victory—or I shall not live to see the end."

When World War I started in 1914, the streets of Berlin were thronged with crowds. Now the streets were almost empty. The Germans suddenly saw that their grubby little hero had led them straight down the path to war.

"If we lose this war," said Hermann Goering, "may God help us."

The Early Days of Victory, 1939–1942

ADOLF HITLER had put on his soldier's tunic, and his war had begun. But there was something curiously unreal about the role he was playing. Here he was—the feared German dictator—the great war lord, but in his simple Nazi uniform, with a cap too large for him, he looked like a petty customs officer. That was just what he had wanted to avoid many years ago when his father tried to get him to go into the civil service.

Kaiser Wilhelm II, Field Marshal Paul von Hindenburg, and General Erich Ludendorff, Germany's war lords in World War I, had at least looked the part. They had developed fine scowls designed, much like their pointed helmets, to frighten the enemy. But Hitler, with his puffy face and flabby body, seemed an almost comical figure.

There was nothing funny, however, about the egoism and the hate and the vengeance of this humorless man. He was just fifty years old when the war broke out. He had come a long way since his days as a half-starved rabble-rouser on the streets of Vienna. Now he was the Supreme Commander of the German *Reichswehr*. He already had a few nations under his heel. Soon he would have power over an entire continent.

On September 1, 1939, Hitler's legions moved across the Polish border in the first modern *Blitzkrieg*. There was no declaration of war. The *Fuehrer* hurried to his first military headquarters at the front, in a special train.

Five weeks after the attack, Poland was crushed like an egg between German and Russian forces.

Hitler now wanted an alibi in case the war continued. In a speech to the *Reichstag* on October 6, he offered peace to France and Britain. He did not mention what he intended to do in the future. His one idea was to prepare his own people for a long war. The Germans still could not believe that the *Fuehrer* had led them into another world war.

Then began a period called the *Sitzkrieg,* the "phony," or "sit-down war." It lasted through the winter of 1939. Neither Germany nor the Western Allies attempted an attack. The French stayed behind their Maginot Line, the Germans behind their Siegfried Line. English pilots bombarded Germany with leaflets.

Suddenly, on April 9, 1940, Hitler moved against Denmark and Norway. Within a few hours Copenhagen was surrounded by silent Nazi troops. And within a few days Oslo, Bergen, Trondheim, and Narvik, in Norway, were captured in one great drive. Hitler gave the excuse that he had to invade Scandinavia because the British had laid mines in Norwegian waters. Even if the British had intended to do this, as was most likely, Hitler moved before British mine layers appeared off the Norwegian coast.

There was great joy in Germany. In a mighty blow the *Fuehrer* had done it again! In one lightning thrust he had protected his supply of iron ore from Sweden, taken control of the Baltic Sea, and had placed the whole of the long Norwegian coast at the disposal of his navy and air force. Allied help, mostly British, had come "too little and too late."

Just one month later, on May 10, 1940, Hitler opened his real battle in the west. On the day that Winston Churchill succeeded Neville Chamberlain as prime minister, Hitler sent his fast-moving warriors into Belgium, Holland, and France.

"This battle," he proclaimed, "will decide the fate of Germany for a thousand years."

First came a withering attack by air. The Dutch and Belgians were overrun within a few days. Then, 89 divisions, including ten *Panzer,* or tank, divisions with 3,000 armored vehicles, sliced through the Allied defenses. The

Allies were thrown into confusion. The only good news for the West was the miracle of Dunkirk, where, between May 27 and June 4, 1940, some 338,000 British and Allied troops were taken off the beaches of Normandy in a magnificently staged British evacuation.

All this time Hitler had been telling his fellow dictator, Mussolini, that the British and French were very weak. He promised that both his enemies would soon collapse. On June 10, 1940, therefore, the *Duce* declared war on the Allies.

President Roosevelt commented: "On this tenth day of June, 1940, the hand that held the dagger has struck it into the back of its neighbor."

Prime Minister Churchill used just one word to describe Mussolini's behavior: "Cowardice."

To the surprise of the entire world the battle of France turned out to be a great victory for Hitler. The French army, supposed to be the strongest in the world, collapsed like a house of cards before Hitler's thundering hordes. Actually, the French army was badly trained, poorly armed, and weakly led. Added to this was the effect of treason inside France, and the lack of a will to fight.

When he heard the news of the French collapse, Hitler could not hide his joy. He went almost instinctively into the first step of a Bavarian *Schuhplattler* dance, a kind of jig. A photographer recorded that moment for posterity.

At a clearing in the forest of Compiègne the armistice of November 11, 1918, had been signed by the Germans. A granite block carried these words: "Here on November 11, 1918, succumbed the criminal pride of the German Empire . . . vanquished by the free people it tried to enslave."

Hitler decided to humiliate the French on this very spot. He ordered that the old railroad car in which the World War I armistice had been signed be brought to the clearing.

On June 21, 1940, the area was full of swastikas and excited, joyful German troops. Hitler marched to the clearing, where he entered the railroad car and watched as General Wilhelm Keitel spoke to the French delegates.

Then, not wishing to discuss the details of the surrender (that was for his underlings), Hitler got up and left.

The *Fuehrer* returned to Berlin a conquering hero. Germany was covered with flags and banners. Church bells pealed in every village. The great *Fuehrer*, in just a little over two months, had elevated himself by a series of brilliant military victories to the class of the great Frederick.

Surely, thought the German people, the war would now be over within a few weeks. Who could hold out any longer against the mighty *Fuehrer*?

Once again Hitler turned to the British. See, he said, you have lost your last ally on the Continent. You don't have a chance now. Be sensible. Give us back our colonies. Recognize our dominant position in Europe.

"I can see no reason," he said, "why this war must continue."

The British people, led by Winston Churchill, replied with silence.

But Churchill spoke to the British people: "What has happened in France makes no difference to British faith and purpose. We have become the sole champions now in arms to defend the world cause. . . . We shall defend our island, and, with the British Empire around us, we shall fight on unconquerable, until the curse of Hitler is lifted from the brows of men. We are sure that in the end all will be well."

Hitler waited two weeks and then gave Goering the order to start total war against the British Isles. First came an attack by the *Luftwaffe* to sweep the Royal Air Force from the skies. This would open the way for invasion.

But it did not work. The R.A.F. pilots, most of them scarcely out of their teens, struck back with savage fury at Hitler's great air fleets. On August 15, 1940, the young Britons shot down a total of 180 planes.

Churchill told the House of Commons: "Never in the field of human conflict was so much owed by so many to so few."

Without air power Hitler could not realize his great dream—the invasion of the British Isles, called "Operation Sea Lion." Again and again Hitler had to postpone it—and finally he gave it up altogether.

For a full year England bore the major share of the war against Hitler. Then, in 1941, American aid began to reach England in great quantities.

By this time Mussolini decided that he, too, needed the glory of victory. He sent his Fascist legions across the borders of Greece, but the Greeks fought back. In January, 1941, the *Duce* begged Hitler for help. The *Fuehrer* answered by ordering his troops to smash the Greeks, who succeeded in holding out only for a month.

In May, 1941, at the height of his strength, Hitler made the most critical decision of his military career. He had 250 divisions of German troops and about 100 divisions from satellite countries. General Erwin Rommel was well on the way to conquering Egypt. True, the British had resisted Hitler and had upset his timetable, but he would take care of them later.

Hitler had a new plan now. He would attack his partner, Soviet Russia! After all, his pact with Stalin was only a temporary matter, he reasoned. He must never forget that he, the great Hitler, was the most feared enemy of Red Bolshevism. He would go forth to lead a great crusade. Then surely the stubborn British and the naïve Americans would have to join him in his task of smashing Bolshevik Russia. It would be done in six weeks.

Hitler was always a poor judge of people other than the Germans. Little did he know the caliber of the British or the Americans or the Russians.

On the evening of June 21, 1941, the *Fuehrer* gave a dinner for Russian officials. The next day, June 22, his troops crossed the border and surged into the Soviet Union. There now began a fantastic duel as Germans and Russians clashed along a 2,500-mile front from the Baltic to the Black Sea.

At first, the Germans were successful. They pushed two-thirds of the distance to Moscow in twenty-six days. The Russians, using a strategy called defense-in-depth, rolled with the punch, and retreated. By early October Moscow was nearly surrounded.

"Today," said Hitler on October 2, 1941, "begins the last, great decisive battle of this war."

He was partly right. It was decisive, but in favor the Russians. On December 6, 1941, the day before the Japanese struck at the American fleet in Pearl Harbor, Hawaii, the Soviet armies launched a counterattack. On December 11, Germany and Italy declared war on the United States.

In early 1942, the Russians struck at the Germans with such power that they freed Leningrad from siege and forced twenty German divisions to surrender at Stalingrad.

Meanwhile, Hitler organized his New Order in Europe. To Nazi Germany flowed a huge supply of labor, materials, and money from the captive countries. There were workers from France and Belgium, foodstuffs from Denmark, oil from Rumania, grain and coal from Poland. Europeans watched helplessly as Hitler took their young men, machinery, horses, cattle, and grain.

Hitler's New Order was made up of areas governed in several different ways. First were the countries and areas annexed by the Third Reich: Austria, the Sudentenland, Alsace-Lorraine, Memel, Danzig, Teschen, Eupen, Malmédy, Luxumbourg, parts of Slovenia, and areas of East and West Prussia. Hitler regarded all these as parts of the New Germany. Their people were treated the same as Germans.

Next were the two territories, Czechoslovakia and Poland, neither one taken directly into Germany but looked upon by Hitler as parts of a Greater Germany. The *Fuehrer* had only contempt for these people, whom he regarded as "inferior races."

To the next group of countries Hitler sent his personal aides. He appointed generals to govern France and Belgium.

Norway and Holland were supposed to rule themselves, but Hitler sent Josef Terboven to rule Norway. Terboven was assisted by the collaborator Vidkun Quisling. To Holland, Hitler sent Artur von Seyss-Inquart. He allowed Denmark to retain her own monarch and parliament.

With the European Continent in his hands, Hitler had an opportunity for greatness such as has been accorded to few men in the past. But he made a serious error. Had he offered the defeated nations a dignified role in a new Europe, he might well have been able to consolidate his power. Instead, with lack of foresight, he said his New Order was to be the rule of the master German Race over inferior people.

In the occupied countries there arose resistance movements against Hitler and the Nazis. In France, in Poland, in Denmark, in Norway, in Yugoslavia, in Greece, from one end of the Continent to the other, underground groups made life miserable for Hitler's "Master Race."

Armed bands sniped at Germans from the hills. They sneaked down in the night to derail trains, blow up bridges, clear roadblocks, and explode ammunition dumps. Guerrillas fell on isolated sentries and cut their throats. They knifed German officers and dumped their bodies into the canals and rivers. Factory workers placed sand in the machinery used to make war materials for the Germans.

For the Germans it was as hard to track down this rising resistance as it would have been to place a thumb on quicksilver. The longer the war went on, the stronger became the resistance. Men preferred death to life under Hitler and the Nazis.

Hitler was beginning to learn that winning the first victories did not mean winning the war.

CHAPTER TWENTY-SEVEN 卐 卐 卐 卐 卐 卐 卐 卐 卐

Adolf the War Lord

STEPHEN LAIRD, a correspondent for *Time-Life*, gave a most interesting picture of Hitler in wartime in 1941. Hitler, he said, was now a military conqueror and his whole life revolved around military things. He spent many hours studying military science.

While at Berghof in Berchtesgaden, wrote Laird, Hitler's daily routine hardly changed. Usually, he went to bed about 2 A.M. and hated to get up before 11 A.M. He took his bath in a green-tinted tub and shaved himself with a gold-plated razor. His breakfast was always tea, porridge, wheat toast, butter, and jam. For lunch he ate salad, eggs, fruit, and drank non-alcoholic beer. Dinner was much the same as lunch.

"To get about," continued Laird, "Hitler has a long, two-engined Condor plane, a Mercedes-Benz black touring car, a Mercedes-Benz six-wheeled, field-gray army car, and a special train. All are equipped with radio receivers, and the train has a special car to carry transmission apparatus.

"The Berghof household is run by three women, and all the servants are young married women with children. During the day Hitler walks around a great deal, dictates while pacing, seldom sits long at a desk. For exercise he walks outside, always taking a pocketful of nuts to feed the squirrels. He is a great expert at waiting, living quietly for months, just thinking and planning. Then when action starts he becomes dynamic and seems far younger.

"Besides playing war, Hitler in the past year has found time to look at picture magazines from all over the world; approve the weekly newsreel; edit High Command communiqués; listen to recordings of Wagner's *Meistersinger,* which he calls the ideal expression of Germanism at its best."

With the first Nazi invasion, the Nazi propaganda machine began to glorify Hitler as a great war lord. Hermann Goering on May 20, 1940, said that Hitler had attained heights of military genius achieved only once before in German history—by Frederick the Great. The *Fuehrer,* he said, deserved all the credit for planning and directing the German victories in Poland, Norway, and Western Europe.

"Der Fuehrer," he shouted, "was the man who planned it. In long nights, for weeks and months, Adolf Hitler worked out every phase of military action. He even outlined all minor attacks down to the very last detail."

Goering went on in this vein: "There is no warship, no gun, no weapon in existence that the *Fuehrer* does not know. As an old soldier on the front lines during World War I, he knows the value of manpower. He can also lead armies himself. He knows what is going on all the time. His enormous energy and his sense of discipline make every German officer and private work to the limit of what is humanly possible."

Hitler loved this praise, every word of it. He, too, fancied himself a military master of front rank, comparable not only on the German scene with Frederick the Great, but in world history with Alexander the Great and Napoleon Bonaparte.

Actually Hitler was no military genius, despite Goering's words and his own belief. A shrewd and clever politician, yes, but military genius, no! True, he did have a certain artful, native cunning. a kind of peasant horse sense, that worked to his advantage as a military leader. Until his health began to break at the end of the war he had an excellent memory for details. He learned as much as he could from talking to his generals. But he had a closed mind. He was far too much the product of his own vanity and egoism to become a truly great military figure.

The successful military leader is interested in facts. The ill-educated Hitler relied to a great extent on the so-called science of astrology. Many of his military decisions were based on what his astrologers told him was the position of the stars at any given moment. At other times he depended on his own intuition, which he regarded as infallible. He would "feel" that something was going to happen. When it did, he was sure that the powers-that-be had given him advance notice.

Throughout the war Hitler quarreled constantly with his own generals. The German General Staff was composed of professionals, among them some of the best in the world. They knew military strategy and tactics. These men were trained and educated in the military way of life.

Hitler envied and distrusted men whose education was greater than his. He, the self-educated one, would show them how to win a global war. He would give them lessons in the art of waging war.

At first the German generals opposed Hitler's plans and in private ridiculed him. But in the early days, as the *Fuehrer* won victory after victory, many of the generals began to regard him as a truly great war genius. Few dared now to question his orders or to oppose his strategy. What was the use? He seemed to be right nearly all the time, and they had taken an oath of allegiance to him. To German officers, an oath was a sacred thing.

When France fell in 1940, Hitler, in a rare mood of generosity, announced that he was creating a dozen new Field Marshals. The generals liked that. But as the war went on and Hitler began to lose battle after battle, he tended more and more to blame his generals. It was bad luck; it was the weather; it was the stars; it was the enemy. It was anything—except himself.

Hitler wanted no competition from his generals. In the desert campaign in North Africa there emerged a truly great German military leader in General Erwin Rommel. Rommel had worked himself to the top of his profession by sheer ability. Leader of the famed *Afrika*

Korps, he proved to be so capable and so elusive a tank commander that he was called the "Desert Fox."

Rommel was a hero even to his enemies. British Tommies had begun using the term "doing a Rommel" when something was done just right. Prime Minister Winston Churchill said this of Rommel: "We have a very daring and skillful opponent against us, and I may say across the havoc of war, a great general."

All this annoyed Hitler. He was jealous of Rommel's fame. Still, after Rommel's conquest of Tobruk in June, 1942, Hitler decided it was wise to make him a Field Marshal. Rommel was not overjoyed by the news. "I would have preferred it instead," he said, "if he had given me one more division."

Later Hitler brought Rommel to defend Fortress Europa against the expected Allied invasion of the Normandy coast, which came in June, 1944. Rommel went up and down the whole length of the Atlantic Wall, preparing the defenses, inspiring the troops.

Rommel was no Nazi. He had only contempt for the crude barbarities of Hitler and his henchmen. "They soil my uniform," he said.

On July 17, 1944, shortly after the Allies invaded France, an Allied fighter pilot, by accident, shot up Rommel's automobile on an open road. The Desert Fox was badly wounded.

While in the hospital, Rommel was visited by some high-ranking generals who asked him to join them in a plot on Hitler's life. Rommel agreed that something had to be done to stop the *Fuehrer* in his wild plans that could result only in the destruction of Germany. But he was far too ill to take part in the plot.

The July 20 plot, which we shall discuss later, misfired. Then came a stroke of worse luck. One of the generals in the plot, coming out of the ether after an operation, called for Rommel. He did not know what he was saying. Word was flashed to Hitler at once.

The *Fuehrer* went into his usual rage. Within a few weeks he sent word to Rommel ordering him to end his own life. Rommel, who knew Hitler well enough to fear for his own family, killed himself.

The Nazi press said that Rommel had died of a "brain

seizure." The biggest wreath of flowers at the funeral was sent by the man who had ordered his death.

Hitler was certain that he knew more about war than a dozen Rommels. Yet, two of his techniques played a major part in his defeat—"the Hitler fortress" and the "hold-the-port" strategy.

Whenever he was told that German troops had fallen into an enemy trap, Hitler always reacted in exactly the same way. He would announce that a new "fortress" had been set up on enemy land. It was a strange kind of self-delusion. The man who believed so much in the power of words actually thought that he would change a situation merely by giving it a different name! A wise leader would have ordered his troops to retreat so that they would be able to fight another day. Not Hitler. He made them stay and die to the last man.

In November, 1942, Hitler's Sixth Army, which was attacking Stalingrad, began to stall and break down. It would have been smart to withdraw the Army, let it rest, and build strength for another attack. Certainly there would have been more chance of success if this simple plan had been followed. It was the only possible way of avoiding a major disaster.

But Hitler would not hear of it.

"I won't leave the Volga," he shouted. "I won't go back from the Volga!"

He issued an order:

"The forces of the Sixth Army encircled at Stalingrad will be known as the troops of Fortress Stalingrad."

German troops were starving. Thousands were freezing to death. The wounded were dying because of lack of attention. The rations were cut to the limit. The only encouragement Hitler could give them was to promote their commander, General Friedrich Paulus, to Field Marshal!

In early February, 1943, Paulus and the entire Sixth Army surrendered to the Russians.

"We shall create the Sixth Army anew," was Hitler's only comment.

Similarly, in western Europe, after the invasion of Normandy in June, 1944, Hitler ordered his garrisons to stay on in Brest and other ports along the coastline, long after they were bypassed by the Allies. True, these troops had some nuisance value, but in the long run it was foolish to try and retain a hopeless position. "Hold the ports!" cried Hitler. Such was his vanity that he could admit no error, no mistake, no wrong judgment. The trouble was that his "stars" were not always favorable.

After the war German generals accused Hitler of making two basic mistakes in his grand strategy.

First, they said, he had made the error of not attacking England after the Dunkirk disaster in late May and early June, 1940, when several hundred thousand British and French troops were forced off the Continent by the Germans. Britain was all alone at this time, said the generals. Hitler should have taken the chance of crossing the channel.

Second, said the German generals, Hitler had made another critical mistake by turning on Soviet Russia at the wrong time. In *Mein Kampf,* and a hundred times elsewhere, Hitler had said that he, unlike Kaiser Wilhelm II in World War I, would never make the error of fighting a two-front war, one against the Allies in the West, and another against Russia in the East. He, Adolf Hitler, was too wise for that!

But on June 22, 1941, before making certain that his war with the Western Allies was over, Hitler had turned on Soviet Russia. Soon, like Napoleon before him, he was trapped on the Russian steppes.

Hitler just outsmarted himself, said his disgusted generals.

Table Talk

THE MAN in the rock fortress he had built for himself at Berchtesgaden had one major problem. How could he conquer his loneliness? The war was stimulating. But, oh! the eternal loneliness!

Munching cakes and candies, surrounded by pictures of nudes and stallions and by 7,000 military books, Hitler would talk to his cronies. There were no scholars at Berchtesgaden—Hitler loathed them. There were only the weak-willed, the yes-men, the idol worshipers.

At these all-night sessions high in the Bavarian mountains, or at his headquarters in the East, the *Fuehrer* would hold forth on every subject from food to world politics, from music to war.

These talks were not discussions. Hitler had no taste for hearing anyone else tell his views. He would tell what he thought, and he would supply his own answers.

Much of his talk revealed his colossal vanity, much of it showed hostility and hatred for others, much of it made no sense at all.

Hitler's greatest weakness was that he had an appalling ignorance of the world around him. He might not have attacked the Soviet Union had he not believed his own propaganda. He might have avoided war with England had he not believed his own talk about the "sick democracies." He knew almost nothing about the United States, yet he talked of America like an expert. Had he spent a single day in the factories of Detroit or in the steel mills of Pittsburgh, he might have been more careful about going to war with the United States.

Hitler's unguarded, all-night table talks were taken down in shorthand so that his words could be kept for posterity.

"There was a time," he was fond of saying, "when there was only one Prussian in Europe, and he lived in Rome. There was a second Prussian. He lived in Munich, and was myself."

To Hitler, Germany was the greatest of all countries. "Today," he said, "our movement stands like a rock, and every one of us is ready to fight for it to our last breath. God, who created the German people, has made us strong enough to do this. A nation like Germany riveted together with steel bands cannot be crushed by the ill-will of the whole world. We reach forward a hand of friendship to all those who desire peace, but we will offer a mighty resistance to whomsoever refuses to recognize our independence and denies us equality of rights."

Above all Hitler liked to talk about race. Over and over again he repeated his views about "pure blood" and "superior" races. "It is our duty to arouse the forces that sleep in our people's blood."

"There is only one possible kind of revolution," he would say, "and that is racial. It will always be the same—the struggle of inferior classes and races against the superior races who are in the saddle. On the day the superior race forgets this, it is lost. The Nordic race has the right to dominate the world, and that right will be the guiding principle of our foreign policy. That is why an alliance with Russia, a Slav-Tartar body with a Jewish head, is out of the question."

No one dared to challenge the high priest of Nazism. What he said was taken as gospel truth.

In these talks Hitler took great pleasure is denouncing individuals he did not like. "There's no doubt about it," he said once, "Roosevelt is a sick brain." And on another occasion: "I never met an Englishman who didn't say that Churchill was off his head." It was always the other fellow who was mentally ill.

Hitler's ideas of right and wrong were clearly revealed in these secrets talks. Whatever the Nazis did for Germany, no matter what it was, was right. "We may be in-human!" he said, "but if we save Germany we have re-paired the greatest injustice in the world. We may be immoral! But if our people are saved, we have paved the way for morality."

But it was not all politics. Suddenly Hitler would switch to praise of Richard Wagner's music. "This was German music," he would say. Then he would deliver a lecture on the dirty habit of smoking, the reason why a vegetarian diet was necessary, on the latest advice from his astrologers, on his views about education, on the training of dogs. It was the same Hitler of the Vienna days, of the Munich days, rude and boorish, cocksure, harsh, and vulgar. Success had not changed him.

The record of Hitler's table talks shows a striking lack of wisdom, graciousness, or generosity.

These talks were preceded by hour after hour of mov-ing pictures. When everyone else got tired, Hitler's vi-tality rose. He would talk until three or four o'clock in the morning while his listeners struggled to keep awake. Then he would dismiss them and sleep until noon.

Meanwhile, the war went on.

CHAPTER TWENTY-NINE 卐 卐 卐 卐 卐 卐 卐 卐 卐 卐

The Third Reich Begins to Totter, 1943–1944

IN 1943, Hitler was still strong and powerful. Germany was in the center of what he called Fortress Europa. Surrounding her were such strong points as Norway, Denmark, Holland, Belgium, Spain, Italy, the Balkans. There were some garrisons in western Russia. The German homeland was the main area for making war materials. And to Germany flowed raw materials from the Nazi Empire—oil from the Balkans, iron ore from Norway, minerals from Spain, butter and eggs from little Denmark.

There was fighting in North Africa. Here Hitler hoped to see his *Afrika Korps* drive on to Egypt, take the Suez Canal, and then push through to the Middle and Far East. It was a seesaw battle all the way. But by May 15, 1943, the balance began to shift in favor of the Allies.

Blows now began to rain on the *Fuehrer* from all directions. The British and Americans were plastering his armies in North Africa. The Russians were taking bloody vengeance on the Germans trapped in the Soviet Union. The great days for the strutting little conqueror were over. The Germans were in retreat. From city to city, from village to village, they were being pushed back to their own land.

After the Allied victory in North Africa, came the invasion of Sicily, and then landings on the mainland of Italy. Against hard German resistance, Anglo-American forces reached Naples on October 1, 1943, and Rome on

June 4, 1944. All during this time the Russians were striking furiously at the retreating Germans.

Scores of German cities were being reduced to rubble by blockbusters dropped from British planes at night and by American planes in high-altitude daylight attacks. Early in the war Hermann Goering had boasted: "If a single Allied bomb drops on Berlin, then you can call me Meyer!" Many Berliners now bitterly called him Meyer.

Hitler had started it. People remembered Warsaw and the inexcusable bombing of Rotterdam. Now Hitler was being paid tenfold in kind. In more than five years of bombing, Germany suffered a toll of 305,000 civilians dead and 780,000 wounded.

"Overlord" was the Allied code name for what was to be the supreme event of 1944—the June invasion of the Normandy coast. This was the most remarkable expedition in military history. Never had there been so stupendous an undertaking.

The attack was made with complete initial surprise. Hitler knew that it would come at some time, but just when or where was something he did not know. His defenses in France were quickly broken down. By July, 1944, the flow of troops from the United States reached 150,000 a month, and shipments of war materials about 150,000 tons a month. Britain, too, added her strength.

Soon a million Allied troops were pushing the Germans eastward. They bypassed Paris. They cut the Germans to pieces in a *Blitzkrieg*, a lightning war, unmatched by Hitler in his 1940 drives. By the summer of 1944, six of General Eisenhower's armies were drawn up against Germany's western borders.

And meanwhile the Russians were preparing to open a major drive through Poland toward Berlin.

Hitler was caught in a giant trap. The armies of the Western Allies began moving across the Rhine. The Russians drove relentlessly from the east. The Germans were battered and beaten from both sides. The once proud German armies began to fall apart.

Gone were Hitler's days of glory. Gone were the great victories of the past. Gone was the chance of world conquest. Gone was the Nazi dream.

The Bomb Plot of July 20, 1944

AFTER the war several German historians, in their zeal to remove the odor of Nazism, wrote learned books about the "German Underground" and the "German Opposition." The purpose was to show that many Germans opposed Hitler and the Nazis and that they worked underground to destroy his regime.

Sad to say, this was exaggerated. The record shows that there were indeed, some small and loosely connected groups that opposed the Nazis. But they were never organized into a strong mass movement. Nor were they anything like the strong opposition in Holland, Denmark, Norway, and France, where underground partisans and guerrilla fighters waged ceaseless war against Hitler.

Adolf Hitler was not destroyed by the German people who suffered under his yoke: it took a global union of powers nearly five years to beat him.

On one occasion years before, Hitler had been scheduled to speak at a meeting in a café. A bomb exploded, bringing down the ceiling in ruins and killing a number of people. But Hitler was not there. At the last moment, he had decided to go elsewhere. This just proved, maintained his friends and supporters, that the *Fuehrer* had a "lucky star."

During Hitler's Russian campaign, many German officers were shattered by the extent of the Stalingrad disaster in the winter of 1942–1943. They charged that Hitler lost an entire army by his stubborn policy of trying to hold out at the Volga River. One of them tried to do something about it. A General Fabian von Schlabrendorff, hearing that Hitler was about to return to his headquarters in East Prussia, planned to execute him all by himself.

On March 13, 1943, von Schlabrendorff ordered a member of the crew of Hitler's transport plane to deliver a package to a friend. In it, said the general, were two wrapped bottles of brandy. Actually the package contained a bomb. This same parcel went aboard the plane with the *Fuehrer*.

For some reason the bomb did not go off. Von Schlabrendorff now had a serious problem. How could he remove the evidence? He did it in an amazing way. He flew directly to Hitler's headquarters and by sheer luck managed to retrieve his package. On the way back to Berlin he carefully took the bomb apart and threw its pieces, one by one, out of the window of the train.

Once again the *Fuehrer* had escaped with his life.

Among others who had sworn to kill Hitler was 37-year-old Colonel Klaus-Philip Schenk von Stauffenberg, who had been assigned to staff duty with the Reserve Army in Berlin. Count von Stauffenberg, a member of a noble German family, was a young officer of great personal charm. He had been badly wounded while serving with the German army in Tunisia in North Africa. He had lost his left eye, his right hand, and two fingers of his left hand. Also, he had suffered severe leg wounds.

While in the hospital recovering from his wounds, Count von Stauffenberg did a lot of thinking about what Hitler had done to Germany and the German people. This Austrian, he concluded, had so fouled the name of Germany that decent people everywhere were sick about it. He, Count von Stauffenberg, patriot, loyal son of the Fatherland, was determined to kill Hitler and bring an end to this senseless war that was well on the way to ruining Germany. Then and there, the young man joined the conspiracy against the *Fuehrer*.

The Allied invasion of the Normandy coastline in June, 1944, made it imperative for these plotters to act quickly. Some were already being arrested. On July 11, von Stauffenberg was called to a conference at Berchtesgaden. He brought with him a brief case in which a time bomb was concealed. But that day he did not get the chance to use it.

Four days later von Stauffenberg had a second chance when he was called to the *Fuehrer's* headquarters in East Prussia. This time Hitler was suddenly called away. Failure once again.

Von Stauffenberg resolved that he would not fail a third time.

July 20, 1944. The Russian spearheads were pushing toward German territory. It was a time of great crisis for Hitler, who called a meeting of his top officers at his Wolf's Lair headquarters in East Prussia. Von Stauffenberg was invited to this critical meeting.

It was a sweltering summer day. The meeting was to have been held in Hitler's concrete bunker, but at the last minute the *Fuehrer* decided that it would be too hot there. He shifted to a wooden barrack's room large enough for such a meeting. That decision saved his life.

At exactly 12:37 on that afternoon, Count von Stauffenberg stepped into this room. Twenty-four men were either sitting or standing around a heavy wooden table on which were several war maps. Hitler was leaning over the table.

Von Stauffenberg saluted and said he was sorry to be late. He was supposed to report on the formation of new, front-line divisions of the Reserve Army. Meanwhile, he placed his brief case under the table near where Hitler stood hunched over the maps.

This was no ordinary brief case. Inside it was a cleverly made bomb. Before entering the hut, the young officer had used a little tool to rip the neck of the fuse— a small glass globule containing acid, which bit into a wire spring. The fuse was set to explode in ten minutes.

Von Stauffenberg suddenly excused himself and slipped out of the room. Another officer, finding the brief case in the way of his legs, moved it to the far side under the table. It was a lucky move for the *Fuehrer*. Now there was a wooden table support between the bomb and Hitler.

All this time the voice of one of the officer's describing conditions on the Eastern Front was droning on.

At precisely 12:42 the bomb exploded with a terrific roar. The thin, wooden walls of the hut provided little resistance to the force of the explosion. Windows were blown out. The roof caved in. A hole was blasted in the floor. Thick clouds of smoke and yellow flames rose from the shattered room.

Four men died instantly. Twenty others were wounded.

Panic swept the room. Someone screamed: "Where is the *Fuehrer?*"

There he was, still alive. His right arm seemed to be paralyzed, his right ear deafened, his leg burned. Parts of his trousers were blown off. He was covered with dust.

That afternoon, Hitler, still in a state of shock, insisted upon seeing Mussolini who had come from Italy to visit him.

Hitler told the story to Mussolini:

"I was standing here by this table; the bomb went off just in front of my feet. Over there in the corner of the room comrades of mine were severely injured. Just opposite me an officer was blown through the window and lay outside severely injured.

"Look at my uniform! Look at my burns! When I think about this, I must say I think it obvious that nothing is going to happen to me. It is my fate to continue on my way and to bring my task to its conclusion. It is not the first time I have escaped death by a miracle. There were times in the first war, then during my political career I had a series of marvelous escapes.

"What happened here today is a climax! Having escaped death today in this extraordinary way, I am more convinced than ever the great cause that I serve will be brought through its present perils and that everything will be brought to a good end."

Mussolini agreed: "This is indeed a sign from Heaven!"

News of the bomb attempt sped all over Germany. The *Gestapo* went into action at once to hunt down the guilty officers and their families.

Despite his show of calmness, Hitler was nearly hysterical with anger and rage. He called the plotters "a small clique of criminally stupid, ambitious officers." He intended to have his revenge.

Hitler had all the adult members of the Von Stauffenberg family arrested and executed. He ordered that all the children of that family be taken from their homes and, under false names, given to strangers. As for von Stauffenberg himself and the other plotters—they would be tortured and put to death.

"It is my wish," said Hitler, "that they be hanged like cattle."

And that was just the way they were put to death. They were hanged by the neck with thin piano wires and allowed to strangle slowly. All this was photographed by Nazi cameramen. Hitler stayed up most of one night looking at these horrible moving pictures. He ordered that they be run again and again so that he could relish every moment.

For those who survived the assassination plot in the barrack's room, Hitler gave a special medal, which bore these words:

HITLER—20 JULY, 1944

One of the plotters, a General von Tresckow, took his own life on July 21 to escape the Nazi executioners. He left these words: "My conviction is still firm as a rock that we have done right. I hold Hitler to be not only the arch-enemy of Germany, but the arch-enemy of the world. When I appear in a few hours before the throne of God to render account for my deeds and my omissions, I believe I will be able to answer with good conscience for all that I have done in the struggle against Hitler."

Hitler's Inferno

As THE Allied armies surged into Germany, they revealed to all the world a most shocking crime.

Millions of people knew that Hitler had hated such "racially inferior people" as Jews, Poles, Czechs, and others. They had heard him say again and again that his "pure-blooded Aryan stock" would control the world.

But—that Hitler would seek to murder all these people was just too much for any civilized mind to grasp. Nevertheless, that was exactly what he had tried to do.

All over Germany—in such places as Dachau, Auschwitz, Belsen, and Buchenwald—the *Fuehrer* had set up "concentration camps." These pestholes soon became extermination camps.

It was a terrible human slaughter. As many as 10,000,000 people—the exact number will never be known—were put to death in these camps. They included not only men, but women and children. About 6,000,000 Jews died in this mass murder. To accomplish this incredible extermination, Nazi underlings used devilish methods—gassing, shooting, hanging, starvation, poisoning.

This was Hitler's Inferno—a hell on earth that he himself had created and for which he alone was responsible. Throughout all history, nothing quite like it has ever taken place.

Allied troops who marched into these camps could not believe their eyes. Toughened combat veterans, used to the sights and smells of the battlefield, were sickened by what they saw. There were thousands of bodies piled up like cordwood. Piles of shoes, hair, gold teeth. Gas chambers made to look like shower rooms. And staggering out to meet them were the walking skeletons, crippled by disease and starvation. These were the lucky ones—the ones who had survived.

General Dwight D. Eisenhower, who saw his first death-camp near a town called Gotha, said that he "had never had an equal sense of shock." He went over the entire camp, visiting every corner so he could testify that this was not just propaganda.

Gradually the details emerged for all the world to know:

—Camp guards had bleached human skulls for souvenirs and used the skin of prisoners to make lampshades, handbags, and gloves.

—Corpses had been sent to barbers who removed the hair; to dentists who extracted gold from the teeth.

—Thousands had been put to death each day while loud speakers played beautiful classical music.

—Prisoners had been used by Nazi doctors for medical experiments. Some had been injected with gasoline to see how long it would take them to die. Others had been placed in ice-cold water to determine how quickly they would freeze to death. Others had been shot, and dirty rags forced into their open wounds so that new drugs could be tested.

—At Auschwitz a poisonous gas called Cyclon B, used for killing vermin, had been used to destroy the unfortunate inmates.

Rudolf Hoess, commandant of Auschwitz, told this horrible story before he was hanged:

"On the platform, the Jews were taken over from the police by a detachment from the camp and were brought by the commander of the protective custody camp in two sections to the 'bunker,' as the extermination building was called. Their luggage was left on the platform whence it was taken to the sorting office. . . .

"The Jews were then made to undress near the bunker, after they had been told that they had to go into the room in order to be deloused.

"All the rooms—there were five of them—were filled at the same time, the gasproof doors were then screwed tight, and the contents of the gas containers discharged into the rooms through special vents.

"After half an hour the doors were reopened (there were two doors in each room). The dead bodies were then taken out and brought to pits in small trolleys, which ran on rails. Those too ill to be brought to gas chambers were shot in the back of the neck.

"The victims' things were taken in trucks to the sorting office."

Not even children were exempt from Hitler's hell. They were killed without mercy. They were slaughtered with their parents, and even when they were alone. They were stabbed with bayonets, poisoned, thrown into flames. Thousands died from hunger, torture, and disease.

Edward R. Murrow, the famed Columbia Broadcasting System news reporter, saw the liberation at Buchenwald. "There surged around me an evil-smelling crowd. Men and boys reached out to touch me. They were in rags. Death had already marked many of them. There were 1,200 men in a building that once stabled eighty horses. The stink was beyond all description. I pray you to believe what I have said about Buchenwald. I reported what I saw and heard, but only a part of it. For most of it, I have no words."

A British doctor, Brigadier Glyn Hughes, said this after a visit to Hitler's camp at Belsen: "I have been a doctor for thirty years and have seen all the horrors of war, but I have never seen anything to touch it. . . . No description or photograph could really bring home the horrors that were there outside the huts, and the frightful scenes inside were much worse."

Piles of corpses were lying all over the camp. The huts were filled with prisoners in every stage of disease. There was no sanitation. In one compound, there were 8,000 male prisoners, many with typhus. In one women's compound there were 23,000 women, and many corpses were lying about.

A British officer took films of the Belsen camp. "This film," he said, "will give you some idea of the condition and the degradation to which the human mind can descend. You will see thousands of corpses lying about, and the condition of the bodies. You will also see the well-fed condition of the S.S. who were stationed there. You will see people fishing for water with tins in a small tank. What you will not see is that the water was foul and there were dead bodies in it. That was the only available drinking water. You will see the dead, you will see the living, and you will actually see the dying. What the film cannot give you is the abominable smell, the filth, and the squalor of the whole place, which stank to high heaven."

What did the German people know about these horrible things? No doubt many of them knew nothing at all. The camp guards had to sign papers promising that they would never reveal to anyone the things they had seen inside their camp.

At the same time, many others did know what was going on, or at least had grave suspicions. But so great was their fear that they decided to keep quiet.

Hoess, the commandant of Auschwitz, said: "The foul and nauseating stench from the continuous burning of bodies permeated the entire area, and all the people living in the surrounding communities knew that exterminations were going on at the concentration camp."

Every day trainloads of victims moved in cattle trucks throughout Germany to the death camps. Hundreds of railway workers knew where they were going. In one of the towns near one camp, the local school children would say: "There goes the murder box again." Or one lad would threaten another: "You are crazy and you will be sent to the gas ovens!"

This was Hitler's monument to Nazi efficiency, his legacy to Germany. To describe this mass murder it was necessary to invent a new word, *genocide*. The word is a combination of the Greek *genos* (race), and the Latin *cida* (to kill or exterminate).

Over Dante's Inferno was the inscription: "Abandon hope all ye who enter here."

Over Hitler's Inferno were these ironic words: *"Arbeit macht frei!"* "Work Makes One Free!"

The Last Days of Adolf Hitler

IN mid-April of 1945, Hitler's Third Reich was crashing in ruins. The fast-moving American and British armies were now across the Rhine and heading east. The Russians were driving westward. Germany could not last much longer.

By this time, most Nazi leaders knew that the end was near. They had gambled and they had lost. Panicky and frightened, they began giving themselves up to the Americans and the British—to anyone but the Russians, of whom they were in deadly fear.

But what about the head Nazi himself—Adolf Hitler? Would he go to Bavaria in Southern Germany where his Nazi movement had started? Would he hide himself there in the hills and continue fighting to the last? Where now were the werewolves, those fanatical lads who had promised to fight for the *Fuehrer* until death did them part?

No! Hitler announced to the world that he would not leave Berlin. The Reich Chancellery—that vast, tasteless pile of buildings, which he had built to the glory of the Third Reich—was almost in ruins. Under heavy attack from the air by American and British bombers and from the ground by Russian guns, the Chancellery was now nearly destroyed. There were huge holes in its walls, and the windows were boarded up.

In the garden below the Chancellery, Hitler had built a maze of concrete bunkers—eighteen small and uncomfortable rooms. Here, in what one writer called a "cloud-cuckoo land," Hitler, in the midst of his lackeys, quack doctors, and fortune tellers played out the last act of his life to the tune of Richard Wagner's opera music.

Here, too, in this damp, underground grave, the *Fuehrer* continued to act the part of war lord as if Germany still had a chance of winning the war. He spent hours before giant war maps, shifting colored pins about to locate units that actually no longer existed. With perspiring hands, he shifted maps and papers on the table. He called meetings, gave orders, and barked and screamed at his underlings. He believed he was still the head of a vast army. He continually spoke of depleted units as if they were army corps in full strength. His aides had neither the heart nor the courage to tell him the truth about what was happening.

By this time, Hitler was both physically and mentally sick. Although he was only 56 years old, he was already an old man. He still suffered from the effects of the July 20 bomb explosion. He was troubled by an irritation of the inner ear that affected his sense of balance.

Even worse, however, Hitler had become badly affected by the way he had been living. Shut up in his bunker without fresh air or exercise, he spent much of his time lying on a camp bed between the concrete walls. He could not sleep more than a few hours a night. He ate very little. He complained constantly of headaches and stomach cramps, and refused to take exercise because he believed he had a bad heart.

His face was an ashen gray. He walked with a shuffling, stumbling gait. His hands shook as if he had palsy.

One visitor described him this way: "His head was wobbling a little. His left arm hung slackly and his hand trembled a great deal. There was a strange flickering glow in his eyes, creating a fearsome and wholly unnatural effect. His face and the parts around his eyes gave the impression of total exhaustion. All his movements were those of an old man."

Worst of all, Hitler was slowly being poisoned by a quack named Dr. Theodor Morell. For the last nine years this gross, sloppy doctor had been one of the *Fuehrer*'s closest friends. He had been called in one day to treat one of Hitler's aides and at that time met the

Nazi leader. From then on, he was never far from his new patient. The doctor had profited in many ways. One of his products, an insect killer, which he called "Russian lice powder," had been adopted for use by the German army at Hitler's order.

Hitler was sure that Dr. Morell was the only doctor who could help him. At the least threat of a cold, Hitler, on Morell's orders would take six doses of sulfa drugs. If he was tired, his quack doctor would prescribe strychnine and hormones. In time, Hitler was taking twenty-eight different kinds of drugs—narcotics to make him sleep and stimulants to keep him awake. He carried hundreds of pills of different colors with him munching on them all day.

And if Hitler complained, as he often did, of pains in the stomach, the heart, or the head, Dr. Morell was always there to give him injections.

Other doctors, knowing what damage was being done, protested. But Hitler would have none of it. "You're a bunch of donkeys!" he would shout. "Morell's the only man who knows how to take care of me. You're simply jealous of him!"

Under the care of this doctor, Hitler's health grew worse. He had no actual disease, but he was slowly becoming a physical wreck. His skin was grayer than ever, and his eyes were filmed with fatigue.

The *Fuehrer* now flew from one mood to another. Sometimes he would go into terrifying fits of rage. As one visitor described it: "His fists raised, his cheeks flushed with rage, his whole body trembling, he stood there in front of me beside himself with fury and having lost all self-control. After each outburst of rage he would stride up and down the carpet edge, then stop suddenly before me and hurl his next accusation in my face. He was almost screaming. His eyes seemed about to pop out of his head and the veins stood out on his temples."

"We shall never give up," he would shout. "We shall never give up—never! I have said time and time again—no retreat! We stay where we are! We shall not surrender!"

Then the next day he would fall into black despair, insisting that everyone had deceived him.

What would happen to Germany without him? "I have no successor as *Fuehrer*. The first, Hess, is mad. The second, Goering, has lost the sympathy of the German people. And the third, Himmler, will be rejected by the Party."

Over and over again Hitler shouted that if the war was lost, Germany would die. "We may be destroyed," he cried, "but if we are, we shall drag a world down with us —a world in flames."

Almost to the last day he gave orders to his loyal guards to execute this or that person. It might be one of his old cronies, a doctor, his own brother-in-law, dozens he suspected of treason.

Then, on April 13, 1945, came electrifying news. Dr. Goebbels, who had come to Berlin to stay with the *Fuehrer* to the end, telephoned: "My *Fuehrer,* I congratulate you! Roosevelt is dead! It is written in the stars that the second half of April will be a turning point for us. This is Friday, April 13 . . . It is the turning point!"

Hitler then issued this Order of the Day: "At the moment when fate has removed the greatest war criminal of all times from this earth, Franklin D. Roosevelt, the war will take a decisive turn."

Each day Hitler believed that his war would take a new turn. But it just did not happen.

He held his last war conference on April 22, 1945. Once again he went into a tantrum. He shouted that he had been deserted by his friends. Everybody, he claimed, was lying to him. His generals were no better than so many rats deserting a sinking ship. The whole *Luftwaffe,* Goering's air force, should be hanged. There was nothing left to do but to die. He would take his own life.

Then came another blow. Someone brought him a telegram from Field Marshal Hermann Goering:

MY *Fuehrer:* IN VIEW OF YOUR DECISION TO RE-MAIN AT YOUR POST IN THE FORTRESS OF BERLIN, DO YOU AGREE THAT I TAKE OVER AT ONCE THE TOTAL LEADERSHIP OF THE *Reich?* . . . IF NO RE-PLY IS RECEIVED BY TEN O'CLOCK TONIGHT, I SHALL TAKE IT FOR GRANTED THAT YOU HAVE LOST YOUR FREEDOM OF ACTION. . . . YOU KNOW WHAT I FEEL

FOR YOU IN THIS GRAVEST HOUR OF MY LIFE. WORDS
FAIL ME. MAY GOD PROTECT YOU AND SPEED YOU
QUICKLY HERE DESPITE ALL. YOUR LOYAL
                                        HERMANN GOERING

Hitler exploded into helpless rage. This foul traitor!
This loathsome *Schweinhund!* This fat swine who would
dare to stab the *Fuehrer* in the back and take over his
position as leader of the German people!

So enraged that he could hardly speak, Hitler ordered
a reply. Tell Goering, he said, that he was guilty of high
treason. The penalty for this was death. But in view of
his past services to Hitler, Goering would not be executed. Instead, he must resign all his offices at once.

As if that made any difference now with Russian artillery shells exploding overhead!

The news continued to roll in from the outside—and
it was all bad. One after another the Nazi commanders
were surrendering to the Allies. German resistance was
all but over. The Russians were closing in on the very
heart of Berlin. Shells were bursting in the Chancellery
yard. It was now only a matter of time before the collapse of the Third Reich.

On April 29, 1945, Hitler learned that the Russians
were advancing through a subway tunnel under the river
Spree. He gave orders at once to flood the subway.

One of his aides was horrified. "But my *Fuehrer,*
wounded soldiers of our own have taken refuge there!"

"So much the worse."

The order was carried out. A flood engulfed both the
wounded Germans and the invading Russians. The only
Germans still fighting were boys who were still in their
teens—the Hitler Youth. These lads were defending
themselves with rifles and revolvers against Russian
tanks, artillery, and planes. It was no contest. Out of
5,000 boys, only 500 were still alive.

On the next to the last day of his life, Hitler made his
will. He left all that he owned to the Nazi Party. He gave
his art collection to his home town, Braunau.

"I myself," he wrote, "in order to escape the disgrace
of capture, choose death."

He could not resist one final speech. This time he put

it down on paper in what was called his "political testament." For thirty years, he said, he had been moved by love and loyalty to the German people. It was a lie, he wrote, that he had wanted war in 1939.

"The war," said Hitler, "was started by the Jews." He himself would not leave Berlin.

"I die with a happy heart," he said.

In the second part of his political testament, Hitler expelled Goering and Himmler from the Nazi Party. He named Admiral Karl Doenitz as the man to succeed him as ruler of the Reich. And once again he went back to the theme of his entire career: He begged the new leaders to carry on his struggle against the Jews.

Just before working on these final papers, Hitler did an astonishing thing. He had never married because he had felt that married life would stand in the way of his political mission. He could not, he had said, love Germany and a wife at the same time.

But for many years Hitler had been friendly with a young woman, Eva Braun, who had been content to remain in the background of the *Fuehrer*'s life. She worshiped "her Adolf." On April 15, Eva made her way to the underground bunker. Hitler begged her to leave. Those who were staying, he said, were going to kill themselves.

Eva Braun refused. She would stay with the *Fuehrer* to the very end.

Hitler was touched with this devotion. Since he now had nothing to lose, he decided to marry her. Then they could die together as man and wife.

On April 29, 1945, in that underground madhouse, to the tune of Richard Wagner's music, Adolf Hitler and Eva Braun were married in a simple ceremony. Both swore that they were pure-blooded Aryans.

Herr and *Frau* Hitler had only one day of life left to them.

The next day Hitler had his favorite Alsatian dog, Blondi, destroyed. He walked through the passageways, shaking hands, saying good-by to all. Then he went to his own suite.

At 3:15 P.M. a single shot was heard by those who had chosen to stay with their leader in the bunker.

Hitler was found lying on a sofa soaked with blood. Next to him lay Eva Braun. She had taken poison.

Dr. Goebbels, too, decided to die with his master. He was, as he had promised, loyal to the *Fuehrer* to the very end. In the bunker with him were his wife and his six children, boys and girls from three to twelve years old. For days they had been singing to entertain their "Uncle Adolf." They had had no fear as long as they were near their "uncle." He had promised them that the good German soldiers were coming to chase the bad Russians away and then they would be able to play again in the Chancellery garden.

Goebbels' wife, Magda, had once said: "Life won't be worth living after Hitler and National Socialism have gone."

The six Goebbels children were given injections of poison. Their mother told them that this was medicine to put them to sleep. Helga, the eldest, guessed what was going on and struggled against the needle.

Then Goebbels and his wife walked upstairs. Goebbels killed himself with a pistol shot; his wife swallowed a capsule of poison. The bodies were taken out into the courtyard and burned with gasoline. The Russians later found the corpses.

After Hitler's death an amazing thing happened in the bunker. Those who were left began to smoke! Less than half an hour after the *Fuehrer's* death, everyone was smoking cigarettes in the bunker. While Hitler was alive no one ever dared to smoke in his presence.

The New York Times reported the following when it received word of Hitler's death:

This marks the end of Hitler and the regime that plunged the world into war and formed the core of the fanatical German resistance that has cost so much Allied blood and effort.

The serious, cold-blooded, and wholly humorless Germans had exalted Nazism into a religion that proclaimed Hitler was only the *Fuehrer* of all Germans, but also their God. . . .

Hitler fell as he was supposed to fall—in the roar and terror of battle amid the crumbling walls of his capital, in the Chancellery that he had built as the seat of his world dominion, and at a moment when the conquering Russian armies were planting their victory banners on the scenes of his former triumphs.

The bodies of Hitler and Eva Braun were never found. Almost at once the legends began. "Hitler escaped by submarine and is living on a deserted isle somewhere." "Hitler got away by airplane and is being hidden until he, like Napoleon, could return for another try at world power." "Hitler is somewhere in the Bavarian Mountains."

All of these stories were interesting, but untrue. The evidence has been sifted carefully and from it emerges the word that beyond doubt Hitler died a suicide in Berlin.

It was an appropriate end to the Nazi terror. The god himself had perished. The temple was destroyed. The faithful, that savage tribe, were beaten and scattered.

CHAPTER THIRTY-THREE 卐卐卐卐卐卐卐卐卐卐卐

The End of a Nightmare

ADOLF HITLER was dead. The Germans had lost their dictator. The Nazis had lost their *Fuehrer*. German youth had lost its poisoner. The occupied countries had lost their slavemaster. The democracies had lost their greatest enemy.

And the world had lost one of the most monstrous human beings who ever breathed. It was a close call. For Adolf Hitler had come as near to world domination as any man in history.

This was in truth an evil man. Cruelty was his inspiration, persecution and torture and massacre were his means, world power was his goal. He built his own monument—a row of death camps stretching across the heart of Europe.

Hitler, of course, will have his place in history. But it will be beside the infamous tyrants. It will be, as one observer put it, beside Attila the Hun, who boasted that, "the grass never grew on the spot where my horse had stood."

People all over the globe were shocked and revolted by the Nazi regime. The civilized world turned against the Germans. Germany, it was said, was not a nation of brave soldiers and honest dupes, but a people who knew exactly what they wanted. World conquest was their aim. Until they were beaten, they had been loyal to Hitler. They had wished this tyranny upon themselves.

Now that the war was over, said these critics, the Germans were singing a song of sweetness and light. Take our hand, *Kamerad!* It was all a sad mistake! There were actually no Nazis in Germany—only Hitler, and he was dead. Why should millions of people suffer because of one madman?

These critics also quoted Winston Churchill: "The Germans are always at your throat or at your feet!"

That was one point of view. There was also another. It held that the great German people were, indeed, held in bondage by a gang of ruthless cutthroats. Millions of "decent Germans," this view had it, were also horrified by the Nazis and their evil deeds. It is unfair, it is said, to blame all for the sins of a few. After all, many good Germans gave up their lives in the struggle against the Nazis.

There will be arguments for many more years as to this problem of guilt. There is no easy answer. What we do know is that the record is clear: It happened in Germany.

In the summer of 1960, just fifteen years after the death of Hitler, a Swedish film producer, Erwin Leiser, presented a motion picture all over Germany. He called it *Mein Kampf*—The Record of a Tyrant. This was a collection of old newsreel clippings and documentary films. It was the real thing—accurate as only the camera could make it. There was no love interest. No handsome heroes and heroines. And no part of the film was less than fifteen years old. Yet every theater showing that film was besieged by the biggest crowds in years.

German teen-agers were thunderstruck. Now they saw evidence of a wickedness such as they had never imagined. There on the screen they saw Adolf Hitler, raving and ranting. Most of these young Germans were seeing him for the first time.

At first they laughed at the scenes showing their parents, faces aglow with excitement, cheering the *Fuehrer* at the Nuremberg rallies.

"Sieg Heil! Sieg Heil! Sieg Heil!" It was the barbaric chant of the Nazis gone primitive in the presence of their *Fuehrer*.

Then horror followed horror on the screen. The teenagers began to cry. This was something about which they had known nothing. Their parents and their teachers had told them nothing of these shameful things. As decent youngsters, they recoiled from the spectacle of destruction, suffering, and cruelty.

This was the legacy of shame Adolf Hitler left to a new, innocent generation of German children.

Hitler's rule was a terrible and almost incredible chapter in history. We must never forget it. *For the sake of decency, for the sake of the world's future, let us never forget it.*

MILESTONES IN THE CAREER OF ADOLF HITLER

April 20, 1889	Adolf Hitler born in Braunau, Austria
November 8–9, 1923	Failure of the Munich "beer hall *putsch*"
January 30, 1933	Appointed Chancellor by President von Hindenburg
March 23, 1933	*Reichstag* makes Hitler dictator of Germany
October 14, 1933	Hitler takes Germany out of the League of Nations
March 7, 1936	Sends German troops into Rhineland, which had been demilitarized by the Treaty of Versailles
March 12, 1938	Announces *Anschluss* (union) of Germany and Austria
Sept. 29–30, 1938	Holds conference at Munich to divide Czechoslovakia
April 28, 1939	Denounces non-aggression pact with Poland
August 23, 1939	Makes pact with Soviet Russia
September 1, 1939	Sends armies crashing into Poland; start of World War II
June 22, 1941	Turns on Russia
December 11, 1941	Declares war on the United States
April 30, 1945	Commits suicide in Berlin bunker

INDEX

"HITLER'S WAR"

From the German point of view and secret Nazi documents never before revealed to the public, here is the whole gigantic drama of the most crucial days of World War II. Bantam now presents the books that individually capture the major personalities and events of the war.

☐ **HITLER AND NAZISM** by Louis Snyder   8047 $1.50

☐ **CRACK OF DOOM** by Willi Heinrich   8041 $1.25

☐ **THE MURDERERS AMONG US**
by Simon Wiesenthal   7593 $1.25

☐ **THE GAME OF THE FOXES** by Ladislas Farago   7477 $1.95

☐ **PICTORIAL HISTORY OF THE THIRD REICH**
by Neuman & Koppel   6705 $1.25

☐ **THE LAST 100 DAYS** by John Toland   5812 $1.65

☐ **EYEWITNESS HISTORY OF WW II: VICTORY**
by Abraham Rothberg   10130 $1.75

☐ **EYEWITNESS HISTORY OF WW II: COUNTER-ATTACK** by Abraham Rothberg   10129 $1.75

☐ **EYEWITNESS HISTORY OF WW II: SIEGE**
by Abraham Rothberg   10128 $1.75

☐ **EYEWITNESS HISTORY OF WW II: BLITZKRIEG**
by Abraham Rothberg   10127 $1.75

Buy them at your local bookstore or use this handy coupon:

Bantam Books, Inc., Dept. HW, 414 East Golf Road, Des Plaines, Ill. 60016

Please send me the books indicated above. I am enclosing $_____ (please add 35¢ to cover postage and handling). Send check or money order—no cash or C.O.D.'s please.

Mr/Mrs/Miss_____

Address_____

City_____State/Zip_____

HW—7/76

Please allow three weeks for delivery. This offer expires 7/77.